BASIC MASONRY TECHNIQUES

*Created and designed
by the editorial staff
of ORTHO Books.*

Project Editor
Jim Beley

Writer
T. Jeff Williams

Illustrators
Ron Hildebrand
Ronda Hildebrand

Ortho Books

Publisher
Robert L. Iacopi

Editorial Director
Min S. Yee

Managing Editors
Anne Coolman
Michael D. Smith
Sally W. Smith

Production Manager
Ernie S. Tasaki

Editors
Jim Beley
Susan Lammers
Deni Stein

System Manager
Christopher Banks

System Consultant
Mark Zielinski

Asst. System Managers
Linda Bouchard
William F. Yusavage

Photographic Director
Alan Copeland

Photographers
Laurie A. Black
Richard A. Christman

Asst. Production Manager
Darcie S. Furlan

Associate Editors
Richard H. Bond
Alice E. Mace

Production Editors
Don Mosley
Kate O'Keeffe

Chief Copy Editor
Rebecca Pepper

Photo Editors
Anne Pederson
Pam Peirce

National Sales Manager
Garry P. Wellman

Sales Associate
Susan B. Boyle

Operations Director
William T. Pletcher

Operations Assistant
Gail L. Davis

Administrative Assistant
Georgiann Wright

Address all inquiries to
Ortho Books
Chevron Chemical Company
Consumer Products Division
Box 5047
San Ramon, CA 94583

First Printing in March, 1985

      6 7 8 9
         89 90

ISBN 0-89721-045-X UPC 05946

Library of Congress Catalog Card
Number 85-060003

Chevron Chemical Company
6001 Bollinger Canyon Road, San Ramon, CA 94583

Acknowledgments

Graphic Design
Jonson Pedersen Hinrichs & Shakery
San Francisco, CA

Photographers
William Aplin: p. 46, 75
Jim Beley: p. 6
Carol Bernson: p. 9 (bottom), 52-53, back cover
  (top right)
Laurie Black: Front Cover, 10-11, 15, 16,
  67 (right)
Josephine Coatsworth: p. 62-63
Dick Christman: p. 20, 21, 22, 44, 45, 54, 67 (left),
  77
Donna Dellario: p. 9 (right)
Derek Fell: p. 58
B. J. Kinkead: p. 84 (right), 90, back cover (bottom
  left)
Michael Landis: p. 3 (left), (bottom), 4-5,
  7 (top), 12 (top), 17, 18-19, 32, 78-79,
  84 (left), back cover (top left)
Leffingwell Associates: p. 12 (bottom)
Michael McKinley: p. 4, 7 (bottom), 9 (top), 56, 57
Ortho Photo Library: p. 8 (top), 13, 14
Anne Pederson: p. 3, 42-43, back cover (bottom
  right)
Emery Rogers & Associates: p. 64
Tom Tracy: p. 8 (bottom), 30
T. Jeff Williams: p. 26

Landscape Designers
Front Cover and Page 16: Royston, Hanamoto,
  Alley & Abey, Mill Valley, CA
Page 3, 42-43, back cover (top right): Richard
  Schadt Associates,
San Francisco, CA
Page 10-11: Frank Lloyd Wright
Page 12 (bottom): Leffingwell & Associates,
  Sausalito, CA
Page 15: Roger Fiske, San Ramon, CA
Page 62-63: Treetop Nursery, Don Webb, Bill Hayes,
  Albuquerque, NM
Page 64: Emery Rogers & Associates, San Fran-
  cisco, CA
Page 77: William Louis Kapranos, San Anselmo, CA

Front Cover:

The pattern of circular bricks creates a strong focal
point in this patio. The large, irregular-shaped stones
contrast with the smooth, geometric-shaped bricks.

Back Cover:

Upper left: A brick-on-sand patio requires no mortar
so is relatively easy to build.

Upper right: A rough stone wall is natural in appearance and so inherently beautiful that it always blends
with its surroundings.

Bottom left: Building a concrete slab is within the
abilitiy of many do-it-yourselfers.

Bottom right: A plain brick patio becomes a showcase
with the addition of a gazebo and curved brick wall.

Title Page:

The squares of brick add color and contrast to this
concrete patio.

Consultants

Dave Cline
Potter Valley, CA

Charles N. Farley
Gary Fletcher
Brick Institute of America
Reston, VA

Richard T. Kreh, Sr.
Frederick, MD

Bob Stephens
Ukiah, CA

Photo Stylist

Front Cover: Milana Hames
Oakland, CA

Special Thanks to:

Francis P. Bowles
Dave Dale
Jane Gover
Doug Hocking, Creative Spaces
John Lumsdaine
Shamrock Masonry
Spike and Sara Schulist
Mr. & Mrs. Van Meurs

BASIC MASONRY TECHNIQUES

THE WORLD OF MASONRY

Masonry projects will do more than almost any other project to improve the usefulness and beauty of your garden or yard. A brick patio, for example, creates an outdoor living area that is ideal for entertaining or just relaxing.

This Ortho book is designed to dispel the mystique that surrounds construction with brick, block, stone, and concrete. You don't have to be a professional to achieve professional looking results with masonry. If you can build a deck or fence, then professional-looking masonry projects are within your capabilities.

This brick patio provides a comfortable outdoor living area for the family and for entertaining.

Masonry:
Brick and Stone and More

Masonry is enjoyable and satisfying, but it can also be hard work at times. Keep in mind that you don't have to do the whole job at once. You can lay out a project on one weekend and start it on the next. On something like a brick or stone wall, you can work as long as you wish, then stop. The project will wait for you.

One chapter you shouldn't skip is Chapter 2 about design. Attention to design will make the difference between a well-built but ho-hum project and one that receives compliments from every new visitor to your home. Nothing looks more amateurish than a yard in which every item was built without considering how it would fit into the overall design. Design considerations are important whether you are adding just one project to an existing yard, undertaking a major renovation of your garden, or landscaping a new yard. The chapter on design will show you how a professional would analyze your existing yard or garden and create a design that adds beauty and useful space to your landscape.

Brick

Brick is one of the easiest materials to work with and provides quick and beautiful results. For the novice, the thought of laying bricks and mortar may seem intimidating, but it shouldn't. A brick-on-sand patio requires no mortar and the results are guaranteed to please you and your guests.

Block

Blocks are ideally suited for retaining walls and other projects where strength is important. Working with blocks, as with bricks, involves stacking each unit in a pattern and securing them in place with mortar. Blocks, however, cost less and take less time to lay than bricks, so are a good choice for the do-it-yourselfer.

This block wall consists of preformed panels of blocks, reducing the need for mortaring. Each panel is two blocks high and five blocks long.

Not all brick projects require mortar between the bricks. A rigid border rather than mortar keeps the bricks in place in this brick-on-sand patio.

Exposed stones called aggregate add an interesting texture to this concrete patio.

Stone

Stonework is another natural for homeowners who want to do their own masonry, particularly if they have access to free stone. These building materials may be the rocks you cleared from around the yard, or hauled from a nearby stream. Because of its irregularities, stone is not as easy to work with as brick, but it is still within the range of any novice who has patience.

Concrete

Some concrete projects, like a sidewalk or stepping stones, are relatively easy, while others, like the foundation for a garage, are more demanding. But even building a foundation is within the capabilities of many do-it-yourselfers. So if you have always wanted to build a garage, vacation cabin, or guest house, but have been stalled by the complexities of the foundation, read on. Consider your needs and your skills, then go ahead.

Just remember, no one ever said masonry was easy. It's hard work, but the results are guaranteed to delight.

These rounded stones set in concrete bring the natural beauty of an outdoor stream to this garden path.

Masonry: A Many-Splendored History

One can imagine that the earliest form of masonry occurred when early humans coated a drafty house made of sticks with mud and let it dry. As our ancestors became less nomadic, they began to develop more permanent structures, and clay building blocks evolved. Adobe blocks, which are simply blocks made from clay and dried in the sun, are the earliest remaining relics of the first masons. Archaeologists in the Middle East have unearthed adobe bricks that were made more than 5,000 years ago. Native Americans of the Southwest built elaborate multi-story houses from adobe bricks. Many of these dwellings are still present in Colorado, New Mexico, and Arizona.

By the time of the Roman Empire, the kiln-dried brick was already in wide use. Drying the brick in the intense heat of a kiln made it much harder than the sun-dried adobe. The Romans built their magnificent palaces with brick and then faced them with marble. Brick remains one of the most ubiquitous building materials in the world, whether used for a house, a curving pathway, or a graceful wall.

Stone, like brick, was one of the earliest materials used in masonry construction, but it had obvious drawbacks. It was heavy, irregular in shape, and difficult to use. Still, the master masons of centuries ago found ways to use it. In Central and South America, the Aztecs and Incas built walls and pyramids from massive blocks of stone cut and fit so beautifully that today you cannot slip a knife blade between the joints. Similarly, the Egyptians built their pyramids from carefully hewn stone.

These stepping-stones are made of concrete poured into depressions in the ground.

Stone has been used for construction in many areas of the world because there was little else available, but that did not diminish the quality of the work. Look at the stone cottages in England, Ireland, and Wales. New England farmers had to clear their fields of stone before they could plow, and then, instead of just piling them out of sight, they used the stones to build graceful stone fences and buildings.

Today concrete plays an increasingly great role in the masonry world. Concrete is a fast, inexpensive, and enduring form of masonry. When concrete is used around the home, such as in a patio, it doesn't have to be a simple slab placed outside the back door. Concrete readily accepts many disguises. It can be colored, stamped with patterns, or laced with a surface coating of pebbles. And if it is block that you are using for a wall, a thin layer of stucco can be used as a covering so that no one need know what lurks beneath that rustic surface.

Above: Stone walls don't necessarily need mortar to make them strong or long lasting. The Incas of Peru were masters at cutting stone to make walls and pyramids that still exist today.

Above left: The brick inserts and curved edges create visual interest in this concrete patio.

Below left: Building a stone wall can be like doing a jigsaw puzzle. This wall in Scotland took a lot of patience and rocks. The result is a work of art.

DESIGN: THE FIRST STEP

Designing your yard in advance, rather than just building on a whim, will make the difference between a routine yard and a distinctive one. An understanding of the basic principles of landscaping will help you achieve a yard that is both beautiful and practical, and not cluttered or empty.

Even if your yard is already established, the design principles should prove valuable. For example, you may discover that the addition of a planter made out of used bricks provides a needed focal point in your garden. Or replacing a straight concrete walk with a curved brick walk makes the entryway more attractive to visitors.

The straight lines of this courtyard and house create a feeling of order and formality in this design by Frank Lloyd Wright.

Design Considerations

Sometimes a small detail can make a big difference in the appearance of a yard or garden. For example, when planning a path from the house to the pool, or from the street to the front entrance, consider a route that wanders a bit, perhaps going around a shrub, rather than a straight route. When contractors are laying out fifty or more houses at a time, they tend to be prosaic and keep such things on straight lines; designing your own yard allows you to be a little poetic.

Designing your landscape can be just as much fun as doing the work. The key is to take your time, study your house and property, and decide what will work best for you.

Design Styles

In thinking about how to alter and improve your landscape, consider the style of your house and your own living style. Is your house colonial, western, saltbox, custom, or standard tract construction? Is it formal or informal? Do you like a place for everything, and everything in its place, or are you more nonchalant? Once you have a sense of your own style and that of your house, you can begin thinking about the style of masonry projects that will enhance them. In the end, your house and grounds should reflect you and your tastes.

Elements of Design

In considering how to draw together the many separate units in your landscape, consider the three elements of design: perspective, form, and sense. You can turn a difficult and uncomfortable lot into a pleasant and relaxing one by changing the perspective with which people see things. The shape, or form, of units in the landscape will alter the mood of the grounds. Your senses, such as sight and hearing, and your desire for sun or shade, are also vital considerations in planning the landscape.

Above: The gentle curve, the edging pattern, and the occasional dark bricks create a pleasing entrance walk to this house.

Below: The clean, simple lines of this brick walk and wall fit in harmoniously with this colonial-style house.

*Different levels create
different perspectives
that add interest to even
a small garden.*

Perspective

Three different people may look at
the same thing but see it differently if
they view it from different perspectives. Looking down on a patio generally gives you a sense of command;
seeing it from the same level makes
you feel directly connected with the
patio; looking up from a lower level
may give you either a sense of security or a sense of being walled in.
Depending on the lay of your particular grounds, you may incorporate
some or all of these perspectives. A
deck or patio, for instance, could be
placed on a hillock in your yard, and
a pathway could lead to lower levels
that put you more directly in touch
with your garden.

Perspective also involves the way
you see the rest of the yard or garden
from your favorite sitting area. What
you tend to focus on most, whether it
is a tree, a flower bed, or the farthest
reach of the lawn, is called the axis of
the landscape.

In a formal garden, the axis of the
landscape is arranged in straight or
geometric lines that draw your attention to one or more specific areas. For
example, a group of prize flowering
shrubs, or a fountain, can be placed
at some distance from where you sit,
and your eyes led to the area by the
arrangement of shrubs, hedges, or
pathways.

In an informal garden, your eyes
are still led to specific and attractive
areas, but it is done very subtly. A
gently curving pathway will lead the
eyes across the grounds, or a particularly attractive shrub can be pruned
to draw the eyes to the view beyond.

A sense of mystery is another as-
pect of perspective. That pathway
leading across the yard may disap-
pear behind a hedge, enticing you to
explore a little. A brick retaining wall
may curve around a hill and disap-
pear, suggesting that there is much
more to be seen.

Form

You are surrounded with forms, whether they are the shapes of distant hills, the straight lines of your property fence, or the spreading arms of a tree in your yard. How you use forms in your yard will play an important role in your own sense of comfort when viewing it. For example, if you have a circular patio, a nearby wall or hedge should curve to complement the patio. When laying out walls or walkways, break up the monotony by putting in curves or angles. But be careful. Too many contrasting angles and curves will give you a sense of unease. Your walls, walkways, and shrubbery should balance each other. Suppose you lay out one circular flower bed, 20 feet in diameter, next to one with an 18-foot diameter. Because there is not enough contrast in size, it will appear that you laid one of them out wrong. However, if you put one 10-foot-diameter bed next to one that is 20 feet in diameter, it will appear planned.

There is also symbolism in forms. Curves are symbols of harmony, epitomized by the ancient Chinese form showing the principles of yin and yang—opposites that complement each other, such as light and darkness, strength and weakness. Circular forms evoke a sense of security. Height evokes a sense of awe, whether it is the terraced bank behind your house or a line of poplars; diminutive forms induce curiosity.

Sense

In thinking about the overall concept of your landscape, you must also take into consideration such things as light, sound, color, and temperature. In planning a patio, for example, you should be particularly aware of how the senses will be affected while you are sitting there. If you live in an area with a hot summer, you will want to locate the patio where there will be protective shade, either from a tree or from the house. You may need two patios, one on the south or west side of the house for use in spring and fall, and one on the north or east side where you can escape the broiling afternoon sun.

You also need to be aware of the prevailing winds when planning a patio. If you can't screen out the wind by placing the patio behind the house, you may do so with a decorative concrete block wall or hedges.

Too many straight lines create monotony in a design. A few carefully placed curves, such as shown with this brick wall, heighten the visual interest and increase the sense of comfort.

Keep in mind also that in the evening, cold air sinks and warm air rises. Placing a patio in the lowest portion of your grounds may prove uncomfortably chilly in the evening.

Masonry patios will also collect great amounts of heat on sunny days. In some parts of the country this may be to your advantage, because that heat will be radiated back to you after the sun sets. In other areas it will prove too hot. A light-colored patio will reflect heat, while a darker patio, such as one made of red brick, will absorb more heat.

Sound is another consideration in planning your grounds. If you live in a congested area, street sounds may be intrusive. A high masonry wall will do much to deflect noise. While local codes or your own sense of taste may dictate against a high brick or block wall along the front of your property, walls with gates on either side of the house will help reduce the noise that penetrates into the yard behind.

Texture is another key element in planning your masonry projects. Your choices will include the rugged look of a stone wall or a brick-on-sand patio, the smooth, clean lines of concrete with exposed aggregate surfacing, or the elegance of a mortared brick walkway. These textures can be balanced against one another, and they will also complement other textures in your landscape, such as a rock garden, the smooth green expanse of a lawn, or the smooth lines of a redwood deck.

This is just enough information to make you aware of the subtle complexities that are involved in planning a beautiful yard. With this background, and trust in your own sense of design, you will be able to plan your grounds in a manner that pleases you, which is what matters. For a more detailed description of how to plan your yard, see Ortho's book *All About Landscaping.*

Before You Begin

In planning your landscape, keep in mind that there will be many separate elements involved, but the end result should reflect balance and cohesion. Individual elements such as walks, trees, patios, lawn, walls, and shrubbery should be planned so they complement each other rather than clash. As you plan a project for your yard or garden, keep in mind the design elements discussed above, and work toward a balance of forces.

In planning your yard, there are three fundamental steps to follow: survey, evaluation, and synthesis. Take these steps one at a time:

Survey

The first task is to assess accurately the size of your property and to note any slopes and hills on it. Start by measuring the outline of the property using a 100-foot tape. Transfer the outline to graph paper, and consider each square either 1, 5, or 10 square feet, depending on the size of your lot. Next, measure the outline of the house and place it accurately on the graph paper by measuring the distance from the property lines to the sides of the house. Follow this by placing the circular outline of all trees and existing shrubbery on your plan. Add all other permanent elements in your yard, such as garage, driveway, walkways, pool, and any existing decks, walls, or patios. Now sketch in any terrain changes, such as slopes and hills. Pay particular attention to any depressions where water collects, because you may have to install drain lines there before laying a patio or walkway. Being able to view the whole of the project rather than the individual pieces is the first step in making it all come together.

If summers are hot, locate your patio where trees or buildings will provide some shade and relief from direct rays from the sun.

15

Evaluation

Once you have a complete picture of your property, you can evaluate it and decide on the image you want the property to project. One part of the evaluation is to note where the sun rises and sets in both summer and winter and how the shade creeps across the grounds during the day. This will help you decide where to locate a patio, whether you want it in shade or in full sun. Without making any specific plans yet, you can begin thinking about how formal or informal the yard will be, and what the primary uses will be—for example, an active yard for children and entertaining, or an inactive yard for gardening and viewing.

Make a rough list of your priorities in building the landscape. What should come first, the lawn or the patio, a retaining wall or a walkway? What you want first and what you need first may not coincide. For instance, you may want a beautiful lawn or patio first, but the lay of your land may dictate that you first install retaining or terracing walls. This evaluation of your yard and your priorities may change as you get underway, but by constantly referring to the evaluation you can maintain a continuity of design, which is the purpose of this preparatory work. It may seem time consuming to draw up these plans and lists, but without them you tend to lose sight of the overall plan.

Synthesis

You now have an idea of what you want the yard to look like, what your tastes are, and how you want to project them into the landscape. The next step is to make actual drawings of how you plan to reshape and design your grounds. Before you do this, make sure you are familiar with local codes and how they will apply to your particular project. These code requirements should be incorporated into the drawings, which you may have to submit to the building inspector's office if a building permit is needed for your project.

You have already made a rough outline of the property site by measuring it and transferring all the permanent elements in the landscape to graph paper. That first effort may have been done freehand, to give you a sense of the grounds, but now you are going to make a more exact drawing from the measurements you have already taken. Take your time with the drawings; it is much easier to make changes on paper than it is to change a driveway halfway through a concrete pour. If you don't already have them, treat yourself to a few basic architect's tools, all quite inexpensive but of great help in making your working drawings. The basic tools you need are drawing pencils, graph paper, drafting tape, a circle template, a transparent 45-degree triangle, an architect's scale, and some tracing paper.

The base plan. With your architect's tools and paper at hand, use the measurements of your property to carefully draw everything to scale on a fresh piece of graph paper. This is the "base plan," or what exists at the moment. Be sure to include all pertinent aspects of your house and yard on the base plan, including doors and windows in the house, fences, trees and their drip line, pathways, water faucets, and any underground utilities. By working on tracing paper laid over this base plan, you are going to design your new landscape.

A brick or block wall can reduce the amount of street noise and increase privacy in your yard.

The first step is to go out in the yard, lay tracing paper over the base plan, and note the shadow patterns from any large trees or the neighbor's house, sunny spots, the prevailing wind direction, wind-free areas, high and low spots, and the views, both good and bad. Note any trees and shrubs you may want to remove or move, and note such things as large rocks that you either will have removed or will incorporate into the plan. Pay attention to any low spots where water collects because you may have to put in drain lines, and that should be one of the first tasks.

The bubble plan. Now go up on the roof, the second story, or a ladder, to see the yard with a different perspective. With fresh tracing paper over your base plan, make what landscape architects call a bubble plan, by drawing rough circles—bubbles—in areas where you want to add items such as patios, decks, flower gardens, and shrubbery. Note the best routes of travel from the house to these areas. As you work—and rework—your plan, you will see the elements begin to flow together.

Back on the ground, outline your proposed patio site or walkways with lengths of string or hose, to give you a clearer sense of its positioning. For a more precise awareness of the plan, drive pegs into the ground and connect them with string. Feel free to move the pegs and string until you have a good feel for how your plan will actually work.

The working plan. Now go back once more to the drawing board, with a fresh piece of tracing paper over the base plan, and draw a detailed working drawing of the total landscape. If it isn't quite right the first time, make more alterations with tracing paper until you are pleased with the results. It's even a good idea to wait a few weeks before you start any construction. As you think about your landscape over the next few days or weeks, you will undoubtedly think of minor changes that you will add to make the results even more attractive and useful.

One final word of advice: If, after all your best efforts, you feel that the whole concept does not come together as it should, don't give up. Ask a landscape architect to visit the site with you and go over your plans. Explain what you are doing, and ask about the hourly rate for such a service. In many cases, an architect will probably be able to pull it together for you in just an hour or two. Once you have a final set of working plans and any necessary building permits, you are ready to start construction.

The different textures of the lawn, brick patio, and wood walk make this an elegant outdoor living area.

BRICK PATIOS, WALKS, AND WALLS

O ne of the many values in working with brick is that you don't have to be an expert to achieve quick and beautiful results. Even a novice can turn an unkempt section of a backyard into a stunningly beautiful brick-on-sand patio in a single weekend. It can be even more fun if you—the expert—supervise while family or friends do the work. Somebody has to be the boss.

Brick projects can add a splash of color, warmth, and charm to your yard. Every yard needs a focal point, and a brick patio is an ideal candidate. You will spend countless leisure hours on a patio. Knowing that you designed and built it makes it all the more enjoyable.

A brick patio is an ideal place to spend a quiet weekend or to entertain guests for a summer barbecue.

WORKING WITH BRICKS

The type of brick you select can affect the overall style of the grounds and set the mood you wish to express. A patio or walk with straight edges and perfectly aligned, bright red bricks adds a sense of neatness to a yard.

On the other hand, a curved brick walk constructed with irregularly spaced, mottled bricks creates a more relaxed mood. An even more natural and pleasing effect can be accomplished by planting Corsican mint between the bricks so that the refreshing smell of mint greets each traveler along the walk. As you can see, the possibilities are endless. Let your imagination roam.

In this chapter, the brick projects requiring the least amount of skill—brick on sand—are presented first. The other projects involve the use of mortar, which sounds intimidating but is actually quite simple. Each project requires progressively more skill, but none is beyond the capabilities of the average person. You will learn to lay a brick sidewalk or patio with dry mortar, lay a brick walk with wet mortar, and finally, lay a brick wall with wet mortar. The use of mortar requires a bit more skill to make the job appear perfect, but don't concern yourself with perfection; just do the project. You'll be amazed at how quickly you gain the skills and how professional your efforts will look.

Visiting the Brickyard

There is a confusing array of bricks available, but once you have briefed yourself on the basic types and qualities of brick detailed here, you will be able to place your order at the brickyard with authority.

Bricks are commonly sold at large lumber and hardware stores and at masonry yards. They can be bought individually or in blocks of 100 or 500 bricks. A note of caution when buying a block of bricks: 500 bricks weigh about one ton, so be sure your pickup truck or trailer can carry that load. You can also have the bricks delivered.

There are more than 10,000 different combinations of brick sizes, colors, and materials, but for virtually all home construction projects, you need only be familiar with some of the basic ones. The types of brick most widely used are building brick, firebrick, and paving brick.

Building brick. Also called common brick or standard brick, building brick can be used in virtually all brick construction projects. It is generally less than perfect in appearance, often arriving chipped, but in most projects the blemishes only add to the rustic quality of the brick. A brick may be solid, have holes in it (called a cored brick), or have an indentation (called a frog). The holes and indentation help lock the brick into the mortar, and the frog should always be placed down into the mortar. Use solid bricks for walks, patios, and caps of walls. Use cored bricks where the holes will not be visible, such as in a wall or planter box.

A visit to a brickyard is a must. There you will see the many choices of bricks available for your project.

Building bricks are divided into three grades of hardness that describe their ability to withstand the elements. These are SW (severe weathering), MW (moderate weathering), and NW (no weathering). Grade SW is more expensive than the others because it is made to withstand the harshest weather. It is recommended for projects in areas with subzero winters, or in any project where the brick will be in contact with the ground, such as retaining walls. Grade MW is somewhat less expensive and should be used in areas that have subfreezing weather but not the severe and extensive cold weather that occurs in much of the northern United States and Canada. Grade NW, which is not designed to withstand any severe weather without risk of cracking, is a good choice for many interior projects but not for outdoor projects.

Firebrick. Easily identified by its yellow color, firebrick is made with a special clay and fired at extremely high temperatures to harden it. This brick is commonly used as a lining for fireplaces or barbecues because of its heat-resistant qualities. When using firebrick, you must use a special fireclay mortar.

Paving brick. Harder than common brick, paving brick is sized especially for use without mortar and is widely used for brick-on-sand patios or driveways.

Top: *Building bricks are the most commonly used bricks for backyard projects. The color, texture, and size of bricks that you select will help create the overall effect desired in your project.*
Middle: *Firebricks are yellow and are able to withstand the high temperatures of a barbecue or fireplace.*
Bottom: *Paving brick is more durable than building brick and is ideal for driveways or patios that receive a lot of heavy traffic.*

There are two other types of bricks with which you should be familiar: used bricks and manufactured used bricks. Used bricks are often desirable because of their warm and rustic quality. However, used brick is generally quite expensive, because you are paying for the labor that went into removing the old mortar. If you can haul used bricks away from a demolition site and clean them yourself, you can save a considerable amount. One caution about used bricks: They are likely to be of low quality, particularly if they are thirty or more years old. Modern bricks use better clays and improved firing techniques, resulting in a stronger brick.

An alternative to used bricks is manufactured used bricks—building bricks made with gray and white splotches to look like used bricks.

Brick Sizes and Colors

Because bricks are not made with great precision, they are referred to by their nominal dimensions rather than exact sizes. Some have a nominal length of 8 inches and a width of 4 inches, but are actually 7⅝ inches long and 3⅝ inches wide to allow space for a ⅜-inch-thick joint. Unless you are doing exceptionally precise work, you needn't worry about this difference. The recommended joint thickness in this book is ⅜ inch.

Bricks are made in "modular" sizes. This simply means that bricks are sized in increments of 4 inches, so that they will fit together regardless of how they are placed. Bricks are commonly 4 inches wide and 8 inches long, so that one brick will fit across two bricks laid side by side. Modular bricks make it simpler for the mason to fit bricks around doors and windows, and make it easy for you to fit walls and patios together.

Virtually all brick colors fall in the range of red, brown, or yellow, but the variations can be tremendous. Except for high-quality facing brick, most brick is not uniform in color, but these irregularities only add to the charm of brick in the landscape.

In addition to the varied colors available, bricks come in different textures. The more common textures include smooth face, stippled face, and matte face. When considering bricks for a patio or sidewalk, choose a texture that will provide a nonslip walking surface. Smooth-faced bricks tend to be slippery when wet and reflect an undue amount of light. The rougher stippled bricks are more difficult to clean and are uncomfortable for anyone wearing high heels.

Estimating Quantities of Bricks, Mortar, and Sand

When estimating the number of bricks needed, whether for a patio or for a wall, the first task is to calculate the square footage to be covered. For a square or rectangular patio, multiply the length by the width to obtain the square footage. For a circular patio, multiply 3.14 by the square of the radius. For more complex shapes,

Bricks with a smooth texture (middle) add to the feeling of neatness and order, while bricks with a stippled finish (top) or a matte finish (bottom) provide a less formal appearance.

first draw them on graph paper, with each square on the graph paper equal to 1 square foot. Then count all the squares that are more than half inside the border of the patio or walk to determine the square footage. Order 5 bricks per square foot, then add 5 percent to the total to allow for breakage.

To calculate the number of bricks in a wall, first figure the square footage. If the wall is 2 feet high and 20 feet long, for instance, you have 40 square feet of wall. In walls, allow 7 standard-sized bricks per square foot. In this example you would need 280 bricks for a single-thickness wall. Double the figure for a wall that is 2 bricks thick. If you were going to cap the wall with 4-inch-wide bricks laid side by side, you would need an additional 3 bricks to cap each foot of wall, or 60 bricks for a 20 foot wall.

Mortar is a mixture of cement, lime, sand, and water. It is available in several different forms. Premixed mortar sacks contain the proper amounts of cement, lime, and sand; you need only add water. Premixed mortar is more expensive than other types, but it is handy for small jobs because it saves time. You can also buy masonry cement, which is mixed with lime. This is cheaper than premixed mortar, but you must add sand and water. For large jobs, it is best to buy all the ingredients separately and mix your own, since proportions will vary depending on the type of brickwork you are doing. One bag of premixed masonry mortar will lay about 40 bricks, and one bag of standard masonry cement, when mixed with sand, will lay 100 to 125 bricks. Sand is cheap, so it pays to mix your own cement.

If ordering sand to mix your own mortar, one ton of masonry sand will lay about 1,000 bricks. If you don't have a truck or trailer in which to haul sand, use 5-gallon buckets or feed sacks. Each bucket or sack of sand will weigh about 100 pounds. To keep dirt out of the sand, store it on sheets of plastic or plywood rather than directly on the ground.

Tools for Brickwork

Although there is a wide variety of tools available for brickwork, you can handle many different projects with only a few of the basic ones. You may already have some in your workshop, such as a trowel, level, and hammer. Having the right tools means more efficiency and professionalism on your part. The list of tools below will help you decide what you need, depending on your particular project. None are particularly expensive, but one note of caution when buying tools: Always buy the best that you can afford.

Brick hammers. A brick hammer has a distinctive head, with one end for hammering, and the other for cutting and shaping brick. The handle is made of wood, fiberglass, or steel with a rubber grip. Some masons prefer the wood or fiberglass handles because they absorb shocks better than steel.

Brick tongs. Brick tongs make it easy to move bricks from one place to another. The tongs will firmly clamp and hold up to 10 bricks at a time without chipping them. Brick tongs can be rented, but compare the number of days you will need to rent the tongs against the purchase price and the number of bricks you will be moving for your job.

Brushes. Brushes are used to sweep bricks clean of dried masonry or cement powder before it hardens and stains the brick. You should have two types on hand: one with soft bristles to sweep fresh masonry joints, and one with stiff bristles to go over bricks and dried masonry joints.

Chalk line. A chalk line is a chalk-coated string that marks a long straight line when snapped between two points.

Chisels. Mason's chisels, also called brickset and bolster, are made of a single piece of steel with a beveled cutting edge, and are used to score and cut brick.

Framing square. A framing square is an L-shaped metal tool used for measuring right angles.

Brick tools

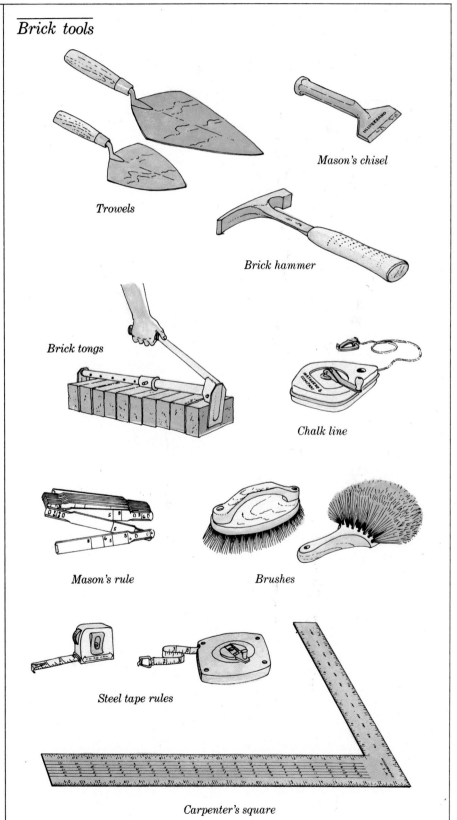

Trowels

Mason's chisel

Brick hammer

Brick tongs

Chalk line

Mason's rule

Brushes

Steel tape rules

Carpenter's square

Jointers. Jointers are used to smooth and finish the mortar joints between bricks, and they come in different styles. The shape of the joint is determined by the end shape of the jointer. A short length of ½-inch copper pipe will also make an excellent convex jointer.

Levels. Choose a level that is at least 4 feet long. Shorter ones will not give you a true enough level when laying courses of brick. Levels are commonly made from either aluminum or wood. Many masons prefer the wood levels because they are easier to clean. All tools must be cleaned immediately after working with mortar, but this is particularly important for the level, since a hardened drop of mortar at one end can result in inaccurate readings.

Line blocks. Line blocks, used in wall construction, are commonly wood or plastic blocks with grooves on the inner edges to hold the mason line. The blocks secure the stretched mason line at each end of the wall and are held in place by tension on the line. There are several variations, as illustrated here.

Mason line. This is a thin but exceptionally strong nylon line that can be pulled taut over considerable distance to eliminate sag. Mason line is used primarily to keep courses (layers) in a brick wall straight and level. Ask specifically for mason line, and don't try to use ordinary string, which will stretch and sag.

Mortar board. After mortar is mixed, place a shovelful or two on a mortar board to be scooped up with the trowel. The board need only be a 2-foot-square piece of plywood with a couple of 2 by 4s nailed to the bottom to raise it off the ground.

Rules. The rules commonly used by masons are special 6-foot folding rules or retractable steel tapes with numbered guides that are used to check the height of brick and mortar joints. In addition to the 6-foot rule, you should have a 25-foot retractable steel tape for laying out patios, walkways, or walls. For large projects, a 100-foot steel tape is useful.

Brick tools

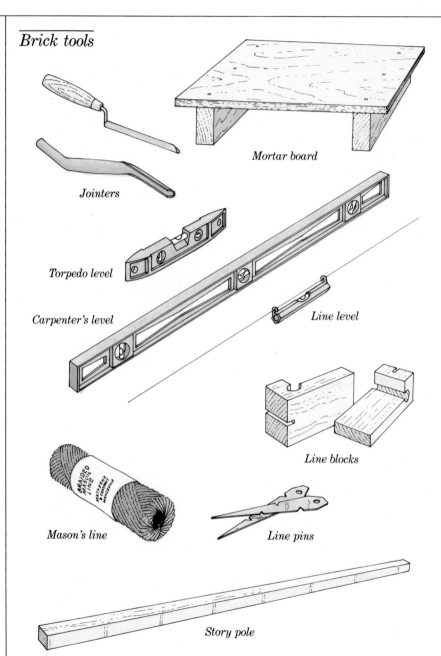

Jointers

Mortar board

Torpedo level

Carpenter's level

Line level

Line blocks

Mason's line

Line pins

Story pole

Story pole. This is nothing more than a straight length of 2 by 2 lumber that has penciled on it the height of each course of the bricks and mortar joints. Place it against the wall periodically to check your work.

Trowels. A trowel consists of a triangular blade that is connected to a wood or plastic handle by a shank. Blades should be made of high-quality steel that emits a clear, ringing sound when struck. Place the point on the floor, and see that it flexes readily. Depending on the type of trowel, the blades range from 9 inches to 12 inches long, and are between 4 inches and 7 inches wide at the heel. For general-purpose use, particularly if you are a novice, choose a trowel with a 5½ inch by 10 inch blade. This allows you to hold mortar closer to the handle, which relieves the strain on your wrist.

How to Cut Brick

If you have ever watched a professional bricklayer at work, cutting a brick looks simple. Many of them just hold the brick with one hand and strike it with the edge of their trowel, and zap!—a cleanly cut brick. In the real world, namely your backyard, use a brickset (a mason's chisel).

To cut a brick, first mark it, then score it on all four sides with the chisel end of a brick hammer or the brickset. After scoring it, set the brick on a firm and level surface, and place the brickset on the scored line. Face the bevel toward the waste section of the brick, then strike the brickset with a single forceful blow. Use the chisel end of the brick hammer to smooth any ragged edges.

Using the brickset generally produces less than satisfactory results, particularly if you want perfectly straight edges or if you are cutting at an angle. It is also virtually impossible to cut hardened bricks with a brickset. The solution is to use a power saw with an abrasive blade. If you have a circular saw, you can buy an abrasive blade at most hardware stores. You can also rent the saw and blade.

To cut a brick with a power saw, mark the place where you want the cut, start the saw, then gently lower the blade onto the brick. Move the blade back and forth over the brick with a minimum of downward pressure. Keep your fingers away from the saw blade. A saw is especially useful when you are laying bricks in a diagonal pattern for a patio, which requires numerous angled cuts along the edges.

A safety note: Working with brick involves virtually no hazards except one—the risk of getting a chip in the eye when cutting brick. This is easily avoided by wearing safety goggles. Keep the goggles handy around your neck or place them in plain view at the brick-cutting site. One other note of caution: When children are around, unplug power tools when they are not in use.

Cutting bricks

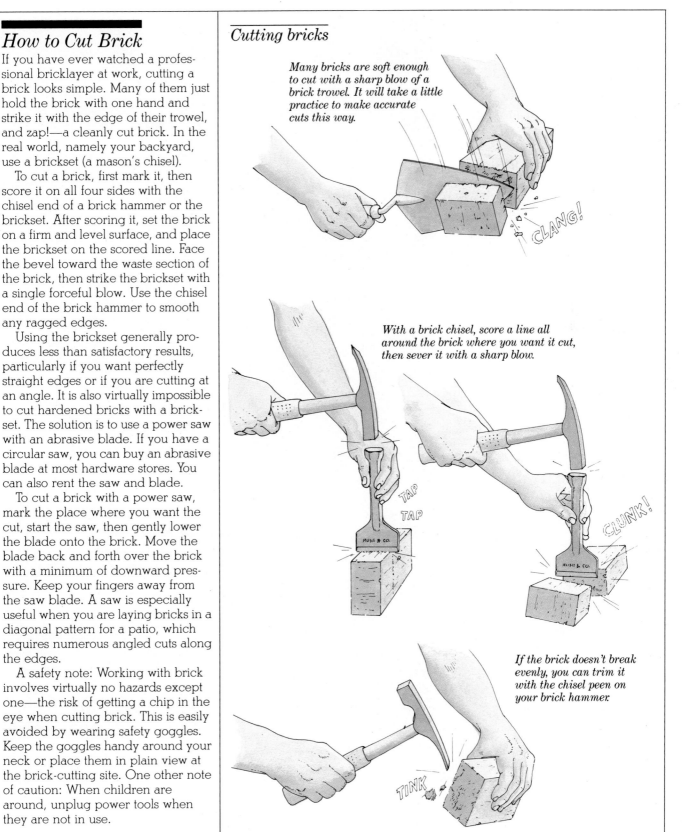

Many bricks are soft enough to cut with a sharp blow of a brick trowel. It will take a little practice to make accurate cuts this way.

CLANG!

With a brick chisel, score a line all around the brick where you want it cut, then sever it with a sharp blow.

TAP TAP

CLUNK!

If the brick doesn't break evenly, you can trim it with the chisel peen on your brick hammer.

TINK

BRICK ON SAND–A PATIO

Laying bricks on a smooth bed of sand is one of the easiest and fastest means of installing a patio, walkway, or even a driveway—and the results can be beautiful.

The key to this technique is to use an edging around the perimeter of the patio. The bricks are laid tightly together within the edging. Sand is swept over the bricks, where it falls between the cracks and forms tiny wedges that keep the bricks in place.

Brick Patio and Walk Patterns

Many of the tried-and-true brick patterns are shown, but before deciding on one, sit down with a view of the yard and think about the effect you wish to achieve. If you decide to combine brick and concrete, review the discussion of design considerations on pages 12–15, so you can successfully combine your brick or concrete patterns with other elements in your yard. For example, if you have a large tree that casts so much shadow that it hampers lawn growth, the spot might be excellent for a brick patio. However, instead of a standard brick pattern, think about a circular one that emphasizes the round swirls of the tree.

The more complicated your brick pattern, the more work you will have to do, but the more eye-pleasing the result is likely to be. Remember that you are going to have to look at your efforts for a long time to come, so take the time to do it right.

Of all the patterns shown, only the diagonal herringbone requires extensive and careful cutting. A power saw and abrasive blade will simplify that chore, so don't hesitate to undertake it, if that is what you want.

The edging of mortared bricks keeps the other bricks in place in this patio.

Traditional

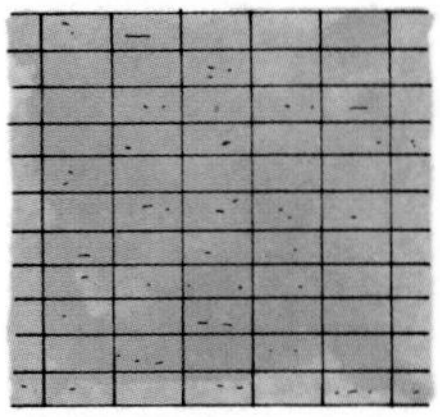

Jack-on-jack

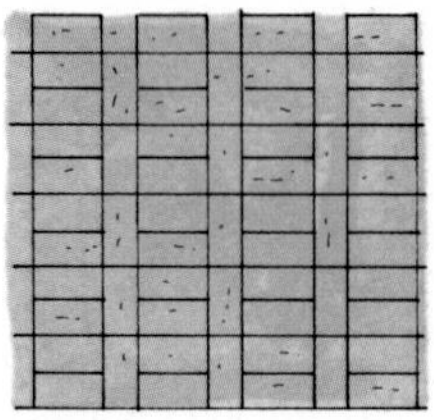

Ladder weave

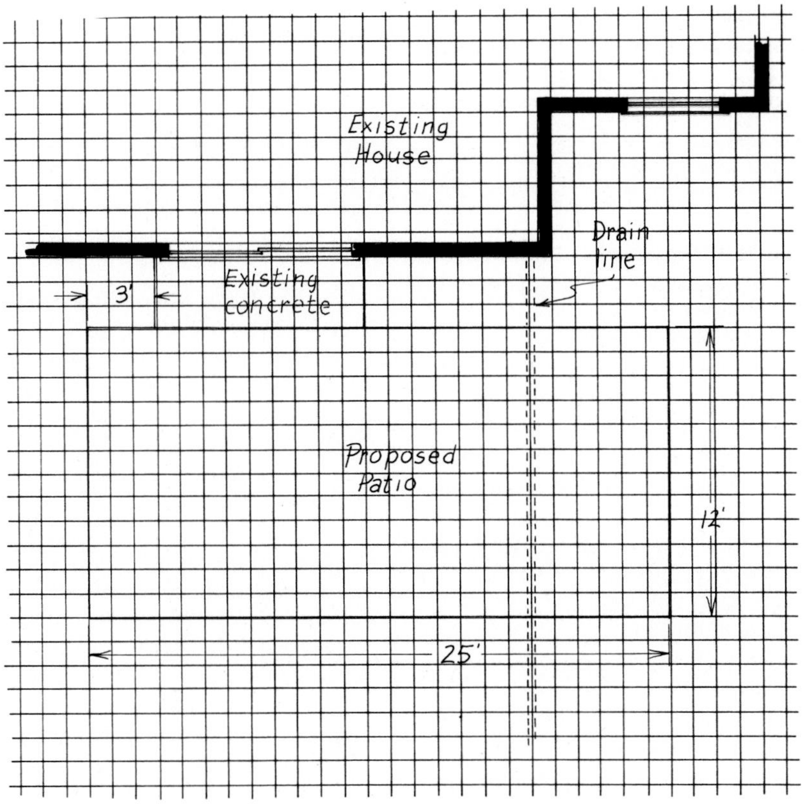

Existing House

Drain line

3'

Existing concrete

Proposed Patio

12'

25'

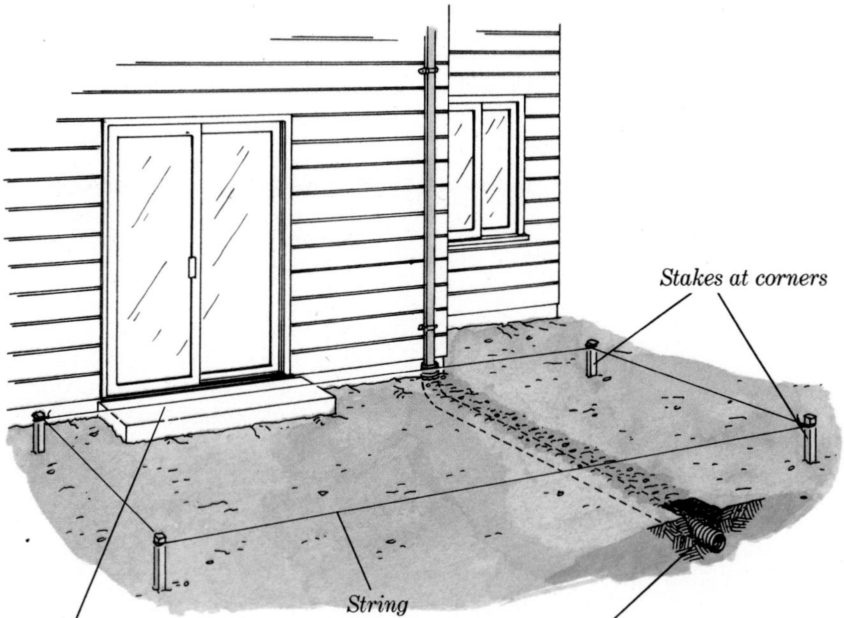

Building the Patio

The first step is to lay out the exact location of the patio. First, drive stakes at the approximate corners of the patio area, then clear and level or smooth the ground within this border. Establish one side of the patio by connecting two stakes with a length of twine pulled tight. If your patio will be square or rectangular, use a large carpenter's square to establish the right angle at this first corner by aligning the string with the square. Repeat this process to carry the string back to the first stake. To check that your square or rectangular patio has true 90-degree angles at all four corners, measure the patio's two diagonals. If the measurements are the same, your corners are square. If not, adjust the stakes until they are. If your planned patio has numerous curves or an irregular outline, you must establish the edging by "eyeballing" it and marking it with a line of chalk or flour on the ground. With the patio outline complete, you are ready to install the edging.

When planning your patio, don't forget to consider potential drainage problems. If the patio is going to be near a drainpipe, install drainpipes under the patio to carry water away from the house. From the illustration, you can see that this is done most efficiently by digging a ditch across the proposed patio site and connecting the downspout to a flexible drainpipe placed in the ditch. If you have no natural drainage area for the water, direct it into a dry well. To construct a dry well, dig a hole 4 feet wide and 4 feet deep, then fill it with rock or gravel. Cover the drainpipe with earth, and you are ready to start the patio construction.

Stakes at corners

Existing concrete

String

Flexible drainpipe from downspout laid in trench and backfilled

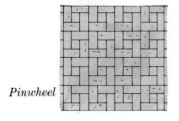

Pinwheel   Basket weave   Half-basket weave

Edgings

Railroad tie

Concrete

Brick in concrete

Bricks on edge

Board

Installing Edging

Since edging prevents a brick-on-sand patio from shifting, it is essential that it be sturdy and long lasting. The three types of edging most commonly used are rot-resistant wood, bricks on end, and concrete. For a concrete edging, see the discussion on page 69. A concrete edging can either be flush with the tops of the bricks, or you can lower it by the thickness of a brick and then set brick edging in the wet concrete.

Whenever possible, make a dry run with the bricks in your chosen pattern to see how wide the edging should be. This will minimize the number of bricks that must be cut to fit inside the edging. On large patios or driveways, you can install permanent edging on two sides and temporary edging on the other two sides. Lay bricks to the temporary edging and adjust the edging until it fits against your pattern, then replace it with the permanent edging.

If the patio is to be raised above the surrounding grade, an excellent choice for the edging is railroad ties. Set them half their thickness into the ground and fill the interior area with sand to within the thickness of a brick from the top. Drill ⅜-inch holes near both ends and in the center of each tie, then drive 3-foot lengths of ½-inch concrete reinforcing rods (called rerod or rebar) through the holes into the ground.

Edging that is flush with the ground can be made quickly and inexpensively from 2 by 4s of red-wood, cedar, cypress, or pressure-treated wood that will not readily rot. To install edging boards, dig a ditch, approximately 5 inches deep, under your string outline. Place the boards with the inside edge directly under the string. Support the boards with 1 by 2 stakes, 12 inches in length, driven every 4 feet and nailed to the outside of the boards. Make sure the tops of the stakes are an inch or so below the top of the edging boards. Use a level to keep the boards level. If a board is not level, don't try to remove the stake—just pry it up or

pound it down until the board is level. When the edging boards are completed, cut off the tops of the stakes at a 45-degree angle and backfill the outside of the trench.

An alternative to board edging is to place a row of bricks on end around the perimeter. Bricks in this position must be set in the ground so their tops will be flush with the surface of the patio. Dig the edging ditch so that the inner face of the bricks is directly under the string line. Use a level to keep the tops of the bricks level. For a much more permanent edging, set the bricks in concrete.

Preparing the Patio Area

With the edging in place, excavate and level the patio area to a depth of about 4 inches. Use a straight 2 by 4 with a level on top to check your work. If the ground is soft and loose, it should be tamped down before you place the sand. You can make an excellent tamping tool from a 4-foot length of 4 by 4 with two handles nailed to the top, as illustrated. If the ground is wet for much of the year, which may cause the completed patio to settle unevenly, excavate it deep enough to place 2 inches of gravel under the sand. Tamping or placing gravel means extra work, but you will have a much better patio.

Adding the Sand Base

Using a shovel, fill the patio area with sand to roughly 2 inches deep. Then dampen and tamp down the sand to provide a firm base for the bricks. The next step is to level or "screed" the sand. The finished sand base must be just the thickness of a brick below the top of the edging. To accomplish this, make a screed board by either notching the ends of a 2 by 6, or by nailing ears on the ends of a 2 by 4, as shown. Level the sand by placing the screed board on the edging and drawing it across the sand. If your patio is too wide for a screed board to reach across it, use a temporary support made from a board staked and leveled down the center of the patio.

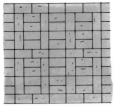
Concentric square

Whorling square

Herringbone

Brick-on-sand patio

After edging is in place, excavate and level the patio area about 4 inches deep.

For large patios, another alternative is to divide the patio into sections with redwood or treated boards that will be permanent. Nail these permanent dividers to the perimeter edging and support them in the center with sand.

Placing the Bricks

Now comes the best part: putting the bricks down. Start from one corner and place the bricks in the selected pattern. Place them firmly on the sand and snugly against each other. Rap them lightly with the hammer handle to settle them. Don't slide them into place because this will create a small ridge of sand between the bricks. To prevent this, place a layer of asphalt-impregnated building felt over the sand before you lay any bricks. Punch two or three holes in each square foot of felt for drainage.

This technique will also keep weeds from growing between the bricks. As you continue placing the bricks, use a straight 2 by 4 to keep the joints aligned, or run a string from edging to edging and use it to keep the brick courses straight.

Put a half-sheet of plywood or some boards on top of the bricks you've already laid to distribute your weight and keep from pushing individual bricks out of place.

Once the bricks are laid, sprinkle a thin layer of fine, dry sand over the bricks, and then begin sweeping the sand back and forth so the grains will work their way into the joints between the bricks. The grains act as tiny wedges to keep the bricks from moving. Leave the sand on the patio for several days and continue to walk on and sweep the patio until the sand works its way fully into the joints.

Screed

Smoothed sand

Temporary support for the screed

Lay bricks on smooth sand.

String

Smoothed sand

Plywood

When bricks are laid in the first section, build a new temporary support and screed the second section.

Sweep sand into spaces between bricks.

SAND

BRICKS WITH DRY MORTAR–A WALKWAY

The beauty of a brick walk need not be extolled at length here; anyone who has seen one is immediately aware of its charm. A brick walk can be laid using the brick-on-sand technique or by using mortar between the bricks.

You should not use the mortar technique on a sand base, since the slightest shifting of sand and brick will crack the mortar joints. To avoid cracked mortar, the bricks should be laid on a flat, smooth concrete foundation. This means you have to either pour a sidewalk first or lay bricks over an existing one.

On these pages, we show you how to build a brick walk using the dry-mortar method. You could also build a brick walk using wet mortar, but this technique is more difficult.

Building the Walk

Building a walk using dry mortar is extremely simple; the process involves little more than laying the bricks out in the desired pattern, filling the spaces with dry mortar mix, and wetting it.

Planning the Walk

First, lay out the sidewalk using stakes and string, as described on page 27 for the brick-on-sand patio. Choose the brick pattern you want and do a dry run to see how the pattern looks in place. If you are planning on laying a distinct edging pattern on each side, be sure to include this in your dry run. Lay out enough bricks to go across the sidewalk and extend down several feet. If you don't like the first pattern, pick up the bricks and try another, until you find one that is right for your garden or yard.

Remember to leave a ½-inch or ⅜-inch space between the bricks. When you are satisfied with the pattern, remove the bricks and begin working on the edging.

Laying the Edge

Edging, either temporary or permanent, must be placed on each side of the walk to hold the dry mortar mix in place until it has been wetted and has set. For temporary edging, cut pieces of 1 by 4 for straight-sided walks, or use bender board for curved walks. Lightly coat the inside of the temporary edging with motor oil, so the mortar will not stick to the wood.

For a permanent edging, use rot-resistant wood (see page 28) or concrete (see page 69). Finish a permanent wood edging with stain prior to installing, then cover it with masking tape to prevent it from being marred or stained by the mortar.

Laying the Bricks

Before actually putting down bricks, sweep the concrete base clean, so the mortar will bond well to it. Lay the bricks according to your pattern, cutting pieces to fit as you go. If you want to be very precise, use pieces of ⅜-inch plywood as spacers. Otherwise, space the bricks by slipping the tip of your little finger between them.

A mortared brick walk is best placed on a bed of concrete so the bricks won't settle and crack the mortar.

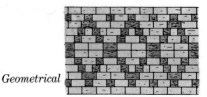

Traditional   **Jack-on-jack**   **Geometrical**

Brick walk with dry mortar

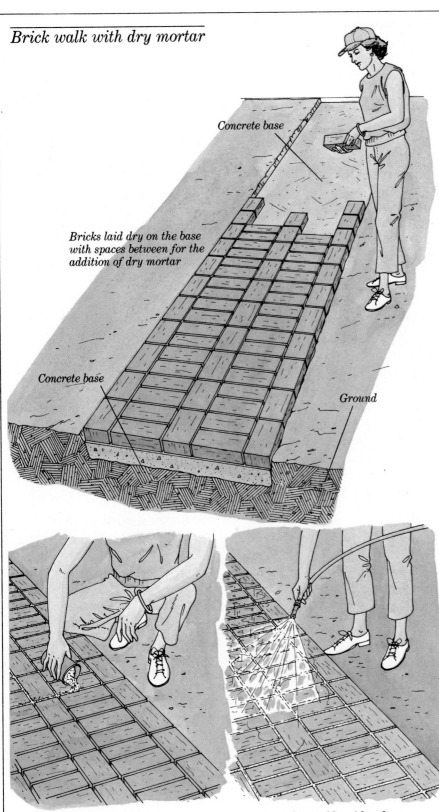

Concrete base

Bricks laid dry on the base
with spaces between for the
addition of dry mortar

Concrete base

Ground

Pour dry mortar into spaces . . .

and wet thoroughly with a fine spray.

Jointer tool

After the bricks are laid out, fill the joints with premixed dry mortar and tamp with a spacer. If you are using temporary edging, pay particular attention to the joints next to the outer edge, so there will be no gaps when the edging is removed. Before wetting the mortar, use a soft brush to remove any that has spilled on the bricks. Wet the mortar with a fine spray, being careful not to dislodge any of it. Wait five minutes, then spray it again to make sure the water has soaked through to the bottom. Some settling of the mortar is likely after wetting, so add more mortar—carefully!—and wet again.

When the mortar begins to set, go over the joints with a slicker or a flat jointer tool. This is important because the mortar will be strengthened by the compression. Tool the short joints first, then the long ones, using smooth, sweeping strokes of your whole arm. If there are some holes that need filling between the joints, mix some mortar in a can and use the jointing tool to smooth it into place.

Cleaning the Bricks

Immediately after tooling the joints, sweep away mortar crumbs with a soft brush. After 12 hours have passed, use a heavy-duty sponge or a piece of burlap soaked in water to scrub away mortar stains.

If you have trouble removing the mortar stains with just water, clean them with trisodium phosphate (commonly called TSP), an industrial-grade cleaning agent available at most hardware stores. Mix ½ cup of TSP in a gallon of water.

If you have really made a mess of it, you can use muriatic acid as described on page 40.

BRICK WALLS

Watching a professional lay a brick wall makes it look so easy. The primary difference between a professional's work and your own, however, is the speed with which it is done.

If you take your time, and work carefully, your finished wall will appear just as good as one built by a professional.

Building a brick wall for the first time means learning some new jargon, a lot of new skills, and gaining new confidence as you complete each step. You will learn that a brick is not simply a brick. It may be a stretcher or a header, or it may have one of several other names, depending on how it is placed in the wall.

Bat. Less than a whole brick.

Bed joint. The mortar under a brick.

Closure brick. The last brick in any course that must be fitted into place is called the closure brick.

Course. One horizontal row of bricks in a wall.

Head joint. The mortar between the ends of adjacent bricks.

Header. A brick laid flat but turned so the end is facing out.

Lead. The end or corner of a wall.

Rowlock header. A brick laid on edge with one end facing out.

Rowlock stretcher. A brick laid on edge so the broad face is exposed.

Sailor. A brick stood on one end with the broad face exposed.

Shiner. A brick laid flat with the wide edge facing out.

Soldier. A brick stood on one end with the narrow face exposed.

Stretcher. A brick laid flat in a wall with the narrow edge facing out.

Wythe. A wythe refers to the thickness of the wall. A wall only one brick thick is a single-wythe wall; a wall two bricks thick is a two-wythe wall.

Before You Begin

Before you actually start building a brick wall, you will need to choose the pattern you want. It would also be a good idea to become familiar with handling wet mortar. A little practice ahead of time will minimize frustrating moments during construction.

Patterns for Brick Walls

Select a pattern for your brick wall from the examples following, or make up a unique pattern to suit your own special needs.

With time and patience, even a novice can build a beautiful brick wall that will enhance a yard or landscape.

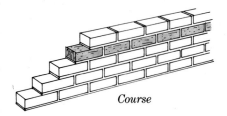

Course

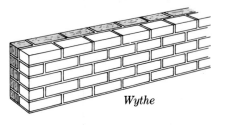

Wythe

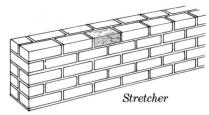

Stretcher

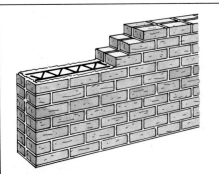

Running bond. This is the most common pattern because it is the easiest. It consists of all the bricks laid as stretchers, with each course offset from the one above and below by half a brick.

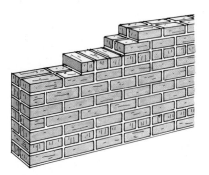

Common bond. Similar to the running bond, the common bond pattern has a course of headers placed every fifth or sixth course.

English bond. This pattern is made by alternating rows of stretchers and headers. Note that the vertical joints of all the stretchers are aligned.

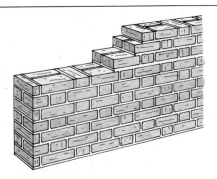

Flemish bond. A variation of the English bond, the Flemish bond consists of alternate rows of stretchers and headers arranged so that the headers and stretchers in every other course are aligned.

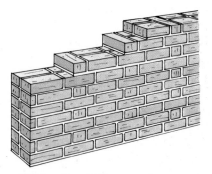

Garden bond. Here, each course has three consecutive stretchers followed by a header.

Stack bond. This pattern has each stretcher stacked directly on top of the one below it. Because it is structurally unsound, it can only be used for a brick veneer, and not as a garden wall or supporting wall.

Know Your Mortar

Mortar is a combination of portland cement, hydrated lime, sand, and water that binds together the masonry units. Hyrated lime makes the mortar more plastic and easier to work. Sand adds volume to the mortar. The sand should be clean and free of stones and dirt, which markedly reduce the bonding qualities of the mortar. You can buy the materials and mix your own mortar, or you can purchase premixed mortar, which is more expensive but saves time. If you buy sand in sacks at a masonry outlet for small jobs, it will be dry, but if you buy sand by the ton, it will be delivered wet. The difference between wet and dry sand affects how much water you must add. If the sand is wet, you will need to add less water than if the sand is dry.

There is nothing difficult about mixing mortar; just be careful to use the correct proportions. Mortar is most easily mixed in a large contractor's wheelbarrow which can then be readily moved about the site as you work. Place the proper amounts of dry ingredients in the wheelbarrow and mix them together thoroughly. Then push the ingredients to one side, add water to the empty side, and gradually drag the dry ingredients into the water with a hoe or a flat-bottomed shovel. A pointed shovel does not work well because it does not pick up all the dry ingredients along the edge of the wheelbarrow. Be careful when adding the last amounts of water, since it is easy to add too much. A good way to test mortar consistency is to trowel it up into a series of ridges. If the ridges appear dry and crumbly, you need more water; if the mortar ridges immediately slump, it is too wet. In a proper mix, the ridges will stay sharp and firm. If the mix is too wet, add some more dry ingredients in the proper proportions.

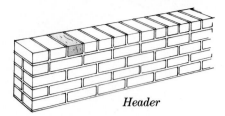

Header

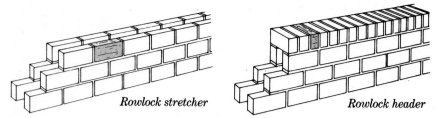

Rowlock stretcher

Rowlock header

Different types of mortar mixes are available. It is important to select the right type depending on the project, location, and climate.

Type M. A high-strength mortar suitable for general use and in walls that will bear a load. Use this mix for any masonry that comes into contact with the earth.

Type S. This is not as strong a mortar mix as Type M. It is excellent for general use, such as a mowing strip, and where masonry will be in contact with earth, unless you live in a region that has subzero winters.

Type N. This is a medium-strength mortar for use above earth where high compression or lateral strength are not required, such as in free-standing brick walls.

Type O. A low-strength mortar that can be used for interior brickwork or where the bricks will be exposed to little weathering and no freezing.

For the projects described in this book, Type N is a good, all-around mortar mix that is strong enough for

Mortar Proportions				
Type	Cement	Lime	Sand	Strength
M	1	¼	3 ¾	High
S	1	½	4 ½	High
N	1	1	6	Medium
O	1	2	9	Low

most yard projects. However, if you are building in an area with subzero temperatures, use Type M.

Because mortar will become too hard to use in about two hours, don't mix more than you can use in that time period. If you see that the mortar is getting a little stiff, you can add some water to return it to a good working consistency. Try not to do this more than twice with one batch.

Bricks: Wet or Dry?
Some bricks, when laid in fresh mortar, will absorb water from the mortar and weaken the joint. Others will not.

Because of the vast variety of bricks, there is a simple test you should perform on your bricks before you begin. Pick any brick at random and pencil a circle on its face about the size of a quarter. Pour ½ teaspoon of water onto the circle, then time the rate of absorption. If the water is absorbed into the brick in 90 seconds or less, the bricks should be wetted before using. The easiest way to do this is to lay out several dozen bricks at a time and spray them on all sides with a hose. Let the surfaces dry before using them because a wet brick will not bond with the mortar.

Mixing mortar

Mix the dry ingredients thoroughly and then add water until the right consistency is achieved.

The mortar is perfect when the ridges stay sharp and firm— no slumping and no crumbling.

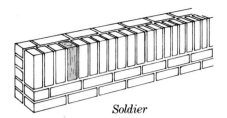

Soldier

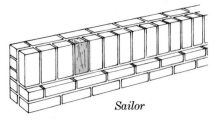

Sailor

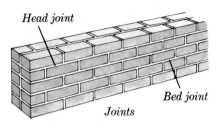

Head joint

Bed joint

Joints

Bricklaying Techniques

If you have never worked with bricks and mortar before, it is a good idea to practice first before actually starting a project. Handling a brick, mortar, and a trowel at the same time will seem awkward at first, but because bricklaying is very repetitive, you will soon feel comfortable at your work.

Mortar is not *placed* with the trowel; it is *thrown.* To practice this technique, first place a shovelful of mortar on the mortar board. Cut a section from the edge of the pile of mortar and, using the trowel, roughly shape it the length and width of your trowel. Pick it up by sliding the edge of the trowel under it in one quick motion. As you pick up the mortar, snap the trowel slightly to bond the mortar to your trowel. That amount of mortar should be enough to bed at least three bricks.

Now comes the part that takes practice: The mortar should be thrown from the trowel in a sweeping motion, with the mortar sliding off the edge of the trowel and landing firmly on top of the bricks. You want to avoid placing the mortar by dribbling it off little by little. This is much slower, and the mortar doesn't bond to the bricks as well. Start by trying to cover two bricks with one throw, then work up to three or four.

Spread the mortar to an even thickness of about 1 inch, then use the trowel to cut off the excess mortar along the edges. You can add that mortar to the bed or place it back on the mortar board. Once the mortar is in place on the wall, lightly furrow the center of the bed with the tip of the trowel. This allows the mortar to adjust to an even thickness as the brick is placed on it. However, do not make a deep furrow, which may leave an air gap under the brick.

After the mortar is spread, the end of the next brick to be placed must be "buttered." Hold the brick in one hand, with the end to be buttered tipped up at a 45-degree angle. Place a small amount of mortar on your trowel, and apply it to the end of the brick with a sharp downward motion. Slapping the mortar onto the brick causes it to bond to the brick.

A brick is not just *put* in place; it must be *shoved.* After buttering the end of the brick, place it on the mortar bed and shove the brick firmly against the one already in place. When done correctly, mortar will be forced out the sides and top of the joint. Skim that excess off with your trowel and use it to butter the end of the next brick. Rap the brick with the end of the trowel handle to set and level it. If a brick is too low, you cannot simply pull it up slightly. This will leave a gap where water can enter, freeze, and crack the mortar. If you place a brick wrong, lift it out, add new mortar, and lay it again.

Bricklaying techniques

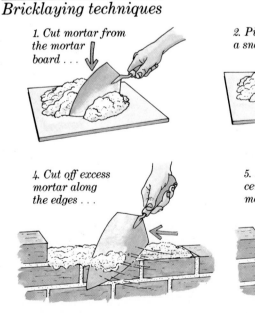

1. Cut mortar from the mortar board . . .

2. Pick up mortar with a snapping motion . . .

3. Throw mortar onto bricks with a sweeping motion, then spread mortar to an even thickness.

4. Cut off excess mortar along the edges . . .

5. Lightly furrow the center of the mortar bed . . .

6. Butter the end of the brick with a sharp downward motion . . .

7. Shove the brick into place so mortar is forced out of the joint.

SQUISH

Building a Single-Wythe Wall

Now that you know how to work with mortar, you are ready to build a brick wall. One of the easiest types of brick walls to build is the single-wythe brick planter box. Normally you wouldn't build a single-wythe wall more than a foot or so high, because it could be knocked over fairly easily. However, once you put corners on such a wall, it becomes much stronger. A few brick planter boxes filled with bright flowers will enhance virtually any yard or garden.

Laying Out the Wall

In this example, we are building a three-sided rectangular box beside a house, with the concrete foundation forming the back wall. Once you have finished the footing for the wall (see page 68), the next step is to lay out the exact position of the wall on the footing. Brush the footing clean of any dirt, so that the mortar will make a tight bond. Center a brick on the footing next to the foundation and make a pencil mark where the outside edge of the first brick will be. Lay a steel framing square flat on the ground, with one edge against the foundation and the tongue next to the pencil mark. Now, using the square as a guide, snap a chalk line on the footing.

Use the square again to mark all the other corners, first marking where the outside edge of the brick will be, then aligning the chalk line with the square and snapping the line. To double check that your layout is square, measure the diagonals. If your work is accurate, the measurements will be the same.

The framing square is accurate enough for a wall that will be 10 feet or less in length. For larger projects, use what is called the 3-4-5 method to make sure your layout is square. Lay out one side of the wall, using the square against the foundation. Measure back 4 feet from the outer end of that first line, and mark the place; this will be the first leg of a triangle.

Building a single-wythe wall

Mark the shorter edges of brick planter with a carpenter's square.

Foundation wall
Brick centered on footing
Carpenter's square
Footing

Mark longer edges of the planter with a chalk line.

Chalk line   Footing

Now stretch the string along the footing and measure 3 feet from the corner to form the second leg. With some helpers, move that string in or out until the diagonal distance between the 3-foot and 4-foot marks is exactly 5 feet. That corner is now a precise 90-degree angle.

Laying the Bricks

With the wall dimensions outlined on the footing, lay the first course of bricks in a dry run (this is called a dry-bond) to see how they fit. Space them with pieces of ⅜-inch plywood, or use the old mason's trick of wedging the tip of your little finger tightly between each one, which will space them almost exactly the right amount. If your footing was laid out correctly, the bricks should fit, but if they don't, adjust the lines on the footing, so you don't have to cut a lot of bricks.

Lay the first course dry with ⅜-inch spacer (or your fingertip) to be sure of the fit.

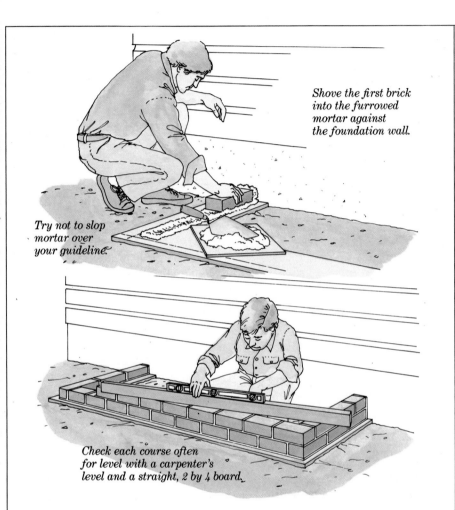

Shove the first brick into the furrowed mortar against the foundation wall.

Try not to slop mortar over your guideline.

Check each course often for level with a carpenter's level and a straight, 2 by 4 board.

Tooling and Finishing Joints

Since you are probably new to brick-laying, you will be working more slowly than a professional would. Thus it is important that you keep a careful watch on the mortar, and tool the joints before the mortar becomes too hard. Joints should be tooled when the mortar will just accept a thumbprint with firm pressure. Tooling the joints compresses the mortar, and is necessary to completely fill the spaces and keep out any moisture. Always tool the head joints first, then the bed joints. If there is not enough mortar in the joint, place a small amount of mortar on your trowel, then pick some of it up with the jointer and press it into the joint.

Tool the head joints first . . .

. . . then tool the bed joints.

Using the troweling technique discussed above, lay a bed of mortar for a distance of four bricks. Try not to cover the chalk line with the mortar. Make a shallow furrow in the center of the mortar. Butter the end of the first brick, and shove it against the foundation and into the mortar bed. Lay the rest of the bricks in this first course in the same manner, then place a level on top to see if any are out of line. If a brick is too high, tap it down with the trowel handle; if one is too low, remove it and lay it again in fresh mortar. Use the trowel to cut off excess mortar on both sides of this first layer, then use the tip of the trowel to smooth and firm up the mortar on the footing.

At the first corner, spread mortar on the footing for three or four bricks again, butter the end of the first brick, and shove it into place against the side of the last brick. Continue laying the bricks down this second side of the planter. Since this leg may be longer than your 4-foot level, place the level on top of a straight 2 by 4 to check your work. For longer walls, use mason's twine and line blocks.

When starting the second course, remember to begin with half a brick, so that this course will offset the first course. The corners of each course will be offset also, as illustrated. In this easy introduction to building a wall, just start at one end of the planter box and keep working your way around, course by course, until you reach the desired height of 1 to 2 feet. Remember to tool the joints before they get too hard.

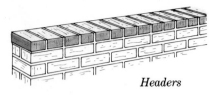

Headers

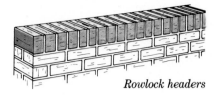

Rowlock headers

Kinds of tooled joints

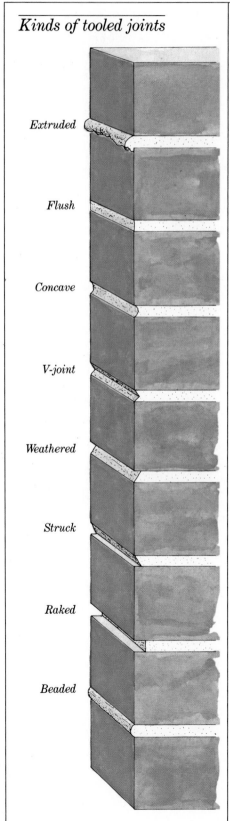

Extruded

Flush

Concave

V-joint

Weathered

Struck

Raked

Beaded

The type of joint you use will affect both the appearance and the lasting quality of the wall.

Extruded joint. Mortar that is forced out between the bricks is simply left as is. The joint is very subject to weathering and should not be used in areas with heavy rain or freezing weather.

Flush joint. Here the mortar is simply scraped off flush with the face of the wall. This method is fast but not recommended for use in areas with heavy rain or freezing weather.

Concave joint. This is one of the most common types of finishes and one of the most weatherproof.

V-joint. Like the concave joint, this one is highly effective at preventing water from entering the joints.

Weathered joint. Here the tip of the trowel is run along the base of the upper brick to cut it back ¼ inch at a 45-degree upward angle. This is the most weatherproof joint.

Struck joint. This is the opposite of the weathered joint, with the trowel used to compact the mortar along the upper edge of the joint. This is essentially weak because it allows water to collect in each joint.

Raked joint. For dramatic shadow lines on the wall, the raked joint is best. Use a special metal raking tool to rake out all the mortar up to ½ inch deep between the joints, or use a piece of hardwood cut to fit between the joints. Raked joints allow water to collect in the joints, and should not be used in areas that freeze.

Beaded joint. This is the opposite of the raked joint. A special metal tool is used to leave a shaped bead of mortar protruding from the joints.

After the joints are tooled, use a soft brush to sweep away loose particles of mortar. Use a large, wet sponge to clean mortar off the bricks before it dries and stains them.

Capping a Wall

Walls are commonly capped for both a finished appearance and to protect them. Walls can be capped with bricks or with contrasting material such as pavers or flagstone.

A common way to cap a wall is with bricks placed as headers or rowlock headers. To do this, lay a bed of mortar on the top course. Then, depending on whether you are using headers or rowlock headers, butter either the edge or the face of each brick and put it in place. This will be a particularly visible part of the wall, so watch carefully that the joint thickness remains constant.

When you are within about 4 feet of the end of the wall, dry-bond the remaining cap bricks to see how they will fit. Since the last brick may extend over the end of the wall, it will have to be cut for a flush fit. Don't place this cut brick last on the cap. Instead, "bury" it 3 or 4 feet from the end where it will not be noticed.

If you cap the wall with flagstone or pavers, use the same principles described above for brick.

Although the mortar joints may be tooled in any pattern you wish, the joints along the cap should be struck with a flat jointer so there is no depression that will collect moisture.

Building Leads

The brick planter box described. above is an easy introduction to laying a brick wall. However, for most walls the corners of the wall—called leads—are built first, and then the bricks are laid on the line between them. Leads are built first so that twine can be stretched the length of the wall to keep each course straight and level.

There are two commonly used types of lead: the straight lead for the ends of walls and the corner lead. The wall shown here is a basic single-wythe corner lead with a running bond pattern.

In laying out the corner lead, remember this rule: The number of bricks in the first course equals the number of courses in the finished corner. If, for example, your wall will be 11 courses high, you will lay out 5 bricks down one leg of the corner and 6 down the other leg.

Paver blocks

Flagstone

Once the lead is built, you will see that it forms stairsteps by half a brick at a time. To make sure that the bricks are all properly placed, place your level or a straightedge against the lead so that it runs from top to bottom. Every other brick should just touch the straightedge. If a brick is out of line, tap it gently into place, but don't move the top or bottom brick.

Since you are laying bricks from the leads toward the center, the last brick laid in each course must be fitted between two previously laid bricks. This is called the closure brick. To properly lay this one, butter the ends of both bricks already laid, then butter both ends of the closure brick. Place the brick directly over the opening and force it down into position. A considerable amount of mortar will be squeezed out, but this is necessary to form a tight seal.

Drainage Considerations

For brick planter boxes, effective drains can be made simply by putting short lengths of cotton clothesline between the head joints of the base bricks. These work like wicks to drain excessive water.

Any wall built next to a bank or along sloping ground may be subject to considerable additional pressure during winter months when the ground becomes saturated. To prevent the wall from being pushed out of line or actually toppled, good drainage behind the wall is essential.

There are two basic drainage systems, depending on the amount of water you expect behind the wall. One system carries the water away from behind the wall; the other lets water drain through the wall.

The first type of drain is excellent on sloped ground and is made by placing rigid, perforated drain pipe, such as is used for septic field leach lines, in a bed of gravel behind the wall. Keep the holes in the pipe down, not up as you would think. This allows the water to percolate up into the pipe and then run down the narrow channel between the two rows of holes.

If the ground is not sloped, drains must be run through the base of the wall. Cut about 1 inch off the end of a brick every 4 feet so a length of ¾-inch plastic pipe can be inserted through the wall.

Extend the pipe about 6 inches into the bank behind the wall and surround it with gravel. Drill holes along the sides to allow more water to enter the pipe.

Fill in the area between, using line blocks and string to guide you.

Line block

String

Line block

"Tail the lead" with a level. The corners of the bricks should line up against a straightedge.

Drainage if base of wall slopes

Drainage through wall if base of wall is level

Brick Problems and Repairs

Although bricks are durable and attractive, they can develop problems. Chief among these are efflorescence, cracked and broken joints, and broken bricks that must be replaced. Of course, careful workmanship can avoid the problem in the first place. But since few of us are perfect, here is how to deal with some common brick problems.

Efflorescence

Few things can ruin the appearance of a brick wall like the gray staining caused by efflorescence. Efflorescence appears usually as a white powder on the surface of bricks, but sometimes it may be a green stain. The stain is caused by water pressure forcing soluble salts from the bricks, mortar, or elsewhere to the surface. The water pressure may originate from the soil beneath a walk or behind a wall, or it may be caused by water that soaked into bricks because of poorly done mortar joints. In the first instance, install drains to remove the water before you clean the bricks; in the second case, a couple of cleanings may do the job.

To clean away efflorescence, first scrub it with a burlap bag or a stiff fiber brush. Do not use metal brushes, because particles of metal will remain in the brick and rust, adding to your stain problems. After scrubbing thoroughly, use high water pressure to wash the wall. If your problems persist, you can wash the wall with muriatic acid. Mix 1 part acid to 10 parts of water, and remember to add the acid to the water, not the other way around. Thoroughly soak the bricks with water first, then scrub the affected area with the solution and thoroughly hose it off. Since the acid may change the color of the bricks slightly, you may want to scrub down the entire wall, or at least wash the surrounding area with a weaker solution to blend it.

Replacing Broken or Loose Brick

A broken or loose brick in a patio or wall is not only unsightly and potentially dangerous, but will also allow water to enter the masonry project and further weaken it. Such bricks should be fixed immediately.

In a brick-on-sand walk or patio, the bricks will sometimes shift or sink in the sand base, which can be hazardous to you and your guests. Before someone trips over a loose brick, pry it up, and the surrounding ones too if necessary, and add more sand. Level the sand and then reposition the bricks. Place a straight 2 by 4 across the repositioned bricks to check that they conform with the rest of the patio or walkway bricks. Sweep more dry sand into the joints when you are finished.

If a brick is broken or loose in a mortared wall or walkway, it must be chiseled out. Use a narrow-bladed cold chisel to remove the mortar and the broken or loose brick. Break the brick with the chisel, if necessary, to speed up the work. Carefully chip away all old mortar on the surrounding bricks, sweep out all the mortar debris, then thoroughly wet the bricks. Do not put in the new brick until the surface of the surrounding brick is dry, or the mortar will not bond properly.

Mix a small batch of new mortar that is most suitable for your climate (see page 34). Butter the edges of the bricks around the opening, and butter the appropriate sides of the replacement brick. Holding the brick carefully to center it in the opening, press it into place. Obviously, a great deal of excess mortar will be forced out, but this is necessary to ensure a tight joint. Clean the edges of the brick with your trowel, then tool the joints when the mortar is just thumbprint hard.

(see page 34)

Replacing a broken brick

Remove the damaged brick and the mortar around it with a cold chisel.

Sweep or hose out the debris and wet the hole. "Butter" the inside of the hole and the edges of the new brick.

Force the new brick into the hole. Clean the bricks and tool the joints to match the old joints.

Cracked Mortar Joints

Cracks in mortar joints are unavoidable over the years, and the causes can range from freezing to settling to simple old age. Careful workmanship at the beginning will delay joint problems, but they are inevitable.

Fixing cracked mortar joints is known as repointing or tuckpointing. It simply means removing the old mortar and replacing it with new mortar. Remove cracked, loose mortar with a hammer and a cold chisel with a tapered blade. Wearing protective eye goggles, cut the old mortar out of the joints to a uniform depth of ½ inch to 1 inch.

After chiseling the mortar out, use high-pressure water to remove all particles of mortar in the joints. If you are working in an area where hosing the wall is impractical, brush the joints clean, then dampen them before repointing with fresh mortar.

Mortar mix for repointing is slightly different than that used for bricklaying. To make it more plastic and thus better able to bond to the old mortar, make the mix from 1 part portland cement, 2 parts hydrated lime, and 8 parts sand. When adding water, a trick from an old pro is to add only enough water initially to make a ball of mortar. Let this mix sit for about twenty minutes, then add more water until it is a rich, plastic consistency ready for application. This rehydration technique will reduce the tendency of old mortar to draw too much water out of the new mix and weaken it. Even so, spray the old brick and mortar with water a few minutes before you start tuckpointing.

When the mortar is ready, place some on your mortar board and apply it with a pointing tool. Fill all the mortar joints in this manner, then finish the joints by using a jointer.

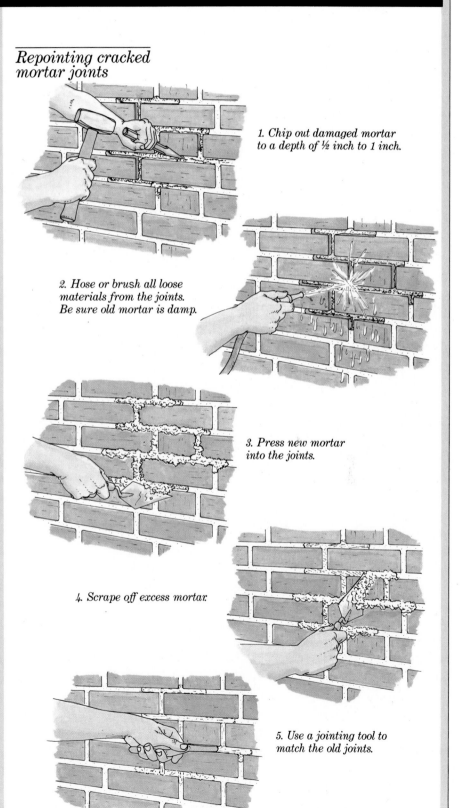

Repointing cracked mortar joints

1. Chip out damaged mortar to a depth of ½ inch to 1 inch.

2. Hose or brush all loose materials from the joints. Be sure old mortar is damp.

3. Press new mortar into the joints.

4. Scrape off excess mortar.

5. Use a jointing tool to match the old joints.

BLOCK WALLS

O ne of the most
common building
materials in use
today is the concrete block.
This versatile item is used
in more ways than you
might imagine, from the
plain concrete building
block to decorative screens
to driveway paving blocks.
Concrete blocks are easier
to use than bricks and go
up much faster. Block is
available in many patterns
and shapes that make it
attractive without a cover-
up, and its low cost and
ease of use add to its de-
sirability as a building
material. If desired, plain
block can also be covered
in numerous ways, such as
giving it a stucco finish
or facing it with brick
or stone.

*The brick cap and stucco
finish enhance the appearance of this block planter.*

WORKING WITH BLOCKS

T*he first step is to visit two or three masonry yards in your area to compare the materials available and their prices. The type and pattern of block that you select will determine the number of blocks you will need for your project.*

Types of Block

Concrete blocks are divided into two main categories: building blocks and decorative blocks. Concrete building block is almost a generic term because the blocks are now made of many different materials. These include cement, cinder, and even such things as shale, clay, or pumice. Cinder blocks are heavy, weighing around 50 pounds per block, while clay or pumice blocks weigh about 30 pounds each, and concrete blocks around 40 pounds.

Building Blocks

Building blocks contain either two or three hollow spaces, which are called cells. The dividers are called webs. The webs and face edges are thicker on one side than on the other. The thick side always faces up and is buttered with mortar before another block is placed on it. Stretcher blocks have ribs at each end, which are buttered and fitted together. At a corner, use the corner block, which has one ribbed end and one smooth end that will be exposed.

In addition to the standard building blocks, you should be aware of the special blocks, such as those with curved ends for a decorative touch on a wall, or those with a solid top used for capping a wall. Other types of special blocks available are those with sculptured faces, those with split faces that look like hand-hewn stone,

or the slump blocks, which closely resemble adobe bricks. Making a wall with any of these types of blocks means you won't have to take extra pains to conceal the blocks.

Standard building blocks are nominally 8 inches wide, 8 inches high, and 16 inches long. All these dimensions are actually ⅜ inch less to allow

for the ⅜-inch mortar joint between blocks. In addition, blocks are sold in widths of 4, 6, 10, and 12 inches. There are also 8-inch square blocks, called half-blocks, commonly used at the ends of walls. The most commonly used blocks for wall construction are the stretcher, corner, and half-block.

Take time to examine all the different shapes and sizes of blocks available. Finding just the right block can make the difference between a ho-hum project and one that elicits compliments from each guest.

Decorative Blocks

Decorative blocks come in a bewildering array, limited only by the imagination and capabilities of the producer. Decorative blocks can be set into solid walls to provide visual relief, or can be used to top a wall, thus making it appear more open. Along with the decorative blocks are the paver blocks, such as the interlocking type shown here for a drive-

Concrete block running bond

way. Other types are open, allowing you to fill the spaces with tamped dirt and lawn seed or flowers.

Block Patterns

Concrete block does not offer the great variety of bonds and patterns that brick does. For virtually all projects, you should stick with the standard running bond. This is not only the strongest of bonds, but is simple and straightforward as well.

Quantity of Blocks

Because concrete blocks are made with more constant dimensions—more so than bricks and certainly more than stone—you can plan quite precisely how many blocks you will need for any given project. Concrete blocks generally don't need to be cut if you plan carefully, particularly in a basic project such as a retaining wall. Instead you buy half-blocks when necessary. You can simplify your own work by designing the project so it comes out evenly. You know that a standard block is 8 inches by 8

inches by 16 inches, so make the wall come out in multiples of 16 or 8 inches. If your project contains openings that do require blocks of different lengths, then cut the blocks to fit, if necessary, with a brick hammer and chisel.

Tools for Block Work

Concrete block work requires relatively few tools, nothing more than what you would use for brick work (see page 23). These include a trowel, 4-foot level, mason's twine, and line blocks to keep the courses straight, and a mortar board to keep the concrete mix close to your work. To finish the blocks, you need to purchase or make a tool from a length of ½-inch copper pipe bent in an elongated S shape. In addition, a pair of cotton gloves is suggested because the combination of wet mortar and rough concrete blocks can tear your hands.

Not all blocks are just plain blocks. Some serve special purposes, like the curved edging blocks, while others come in decorative shapes.

Interlocking paver blocks create attractive patterns. In cold climates, choose paver blocks with beveled edges so the blocks roll slightly, rather than crack, during frost heaves.

A BLOCK WALL

Good site preparation will mean the difference between a professional- or amateurish-looking block wall; it will also mean the difference between making the job easy or making extra work for yourself.

Building the Wall

A footing must be laid first to support the wall, or it will soon crack and list as the earth moves beneath it. The footing should be twice as wide as the block and at least 6 inches thick. Remember to dig the footing ditch below the frost line or to whatever depth is required by your local building code. Lay out the site using the techniques shown for laying out a brick wall on page 36.

Reinforcement is strongly recommended for any retaining wall and indeed may be required by your local codes. The method described in the section below is for walls that are less than 4 feet high, since anything higher than that may have to meet stringent code requirements, possibly including having an engineer design your wall.

The Dry Run

A dry run is essential in laying a block wall. It allows you to find and solve any problems before you start applying mortar, which makes mistakes difficult to correct. As you place the blocks, use scrap pieces of ⅜-inch plywood to space the blocks ⅜ inch apart, the thickness of the mortar joint. Use stretched mason's twine or nylon cord (no 18) to make sure the blocks are aligned, then snap a chalk line on the footing exactly 2 inches away from the blocks. Use this chalk line as a guide, since it will be far enough away that it will not be covered by mortar spread on the footing.

Building a concrete block wall

Dry run of blocks determines spacing.

⅜-inch plywood for mortar space.

Mark position of corner block with a grease pencil.

Snapped chalk line 2 inches from blocks.

A concrete footing is necessary to keep a block wall from listing, cracking, and eventually toppling.

With chalk or crayon, mark the exact outline of each block at the corner or end of the wall so that the blocks can be repositioned exactly later.

Mixing Mortar

Mortar for concrete blocks is similar to that used for bricks but should be a little stiffer to bear the additional weight of the blocks. Use any of the mixes for mortar shown on page 34, but add just a little less water to keep the material stiffer. Mix no more than you can use in about one hour.

Unlike brick, concrete block should not be wetted before mortar is applied. In fact, keep it protected if there is a chance of rain or even heavy overnight dew.

Reinforcing a Block Wall

To reinforce a retaining wall, first lay out the concrete blocks beside the footing ditch in a dry run. Space them carefully ⅜ inch apart, just what the mortar joint will be. Next, drive ½-inch reinforcing rods into the ditch every 4 feet, in the center of where a block cell will fall. After the footing is poured, make sure the rods are plumb as the footing sets up. The tops of these rods need only be even with the top of the second course of blocks, and can be cut to height after the footing is poured. After the successive courses of blocks are laid, place a length of reinforcing rod into those cells and drive it down to the footing. Fill each cell with concrete and tamp with a narrow stick or piece of reinforcing rod to make sure the cells are completely filled.

Laying the First Course

Spread a solid layer of mortar approximately 1 inch thick on the footing for the distance of two or three blocks. Spread the mortar about an inch wider than the block on each side. Place the first block into position and press it down firmly until it rests on a ⅜-inch mortar bed. Use the level to check that it is level and plumb.

Butter subsequent blocks in the first course on one end only, then press into place against the preceding block. Level and plumb each block, and also place the level against the sides of the blocks as you work to check their alignment.

Building Leads

Once the first course is completed, start building the leads, or the corners or ends of a wall. Note that in a straight garden wall, every other course after the first course will start and end with half-blocks. As you begin laying blocks, always place the side with the thickened edges up so the block will hold mortar better. You will quickly get the hang of this because blocks are much easier to pick up this way. Spread a ¾-inch layer of mortar on top of the first course of blocks for a distance of two or three blocks. Note that you spread the mortar on the edges, but not across the webs. Mortar is spread on webs only if you want to markedly increase lateral strength, which is often done on low retaining walls where no steel reinforcement is used.

Reinforcing a concrete block wall

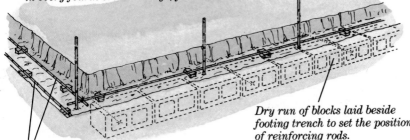

Rerod driven into bottom of trench in line with first hole in every fourth brick—every 4 feet with 16-inch blocks.

Dry run of blocks laid beside footing trench to set the position of reinforcing rods.

Rerod in footing trench raised at least two inches on stones or pieces of brick.

To lengthen rerods, push additional lengths down a cavity beside the first rod and tamp concrete to fill the cavity.

Mortar bed

Check for level and plumb frequently.

Laying blocks

Butter the ends of 2 or 3 blocks at a time.

Set each block in place and tap it gently to line it up with the string.

Butter both ends of closure block and both ends of existing blocks. Hold closure block directly above and push it down in one smooth motion.

As you lay subsequent blocks, butter one end only. Do this by standing two or three blocks on end and buttering them together. Put about ¾ inch of mortar on the ends. Place the block with the buttered end raised slightly, then lower it and fit it snugly against the preceding block in one smooth motion. Use the trowel handle to tap the block level, then use the blade to scrape away the excess mortar that is squeezed out. Mortar that drips on the blocks is better left alone to harden before you scrape it off, since trying to remove soft mortar can result in smears that are harder to clean.

As you build each lead, use the level constantly to check that work is level and plumb. Note also that in a well-constructed lead, you should be able to place a straightedge between the top and bottom block and just touch each block in between.

Laying to the Line

With the leads completed, begin laying the blocks to the line. To keep these courses level and straight, stretch mason's twine or nylon cord even with the top of the course to be laid. Each block should be even with the top of the line and about 1/16 inch (about the thickness of the line) away from the line. Don't let the blocks touch the line. As before, butter the tops of two or three blocks and the ends of a similar number of blocks,

and set them in place. Scrape off all mortar that is squeezed out and work it into the mortar on the board. Make any adjustments of blocks while the mortar is still wet; trying to move a block after the mortar has stiffened will break the bond.

Placing the last block or closure block is the trickiest part of laying blocks on the line. Expertise at this will come only with experience. Butter both ends of the closure block *and* both ends of the existing blocks. Hold the closure block directly above the opening, then push it down with one smooth motion. Immediately scrape off the excess mortar, then tap the block until it is level and straight. If the mortar falls off on your first attempt, pull the block out, remortar everything, and try again.

Control Joints

In long block walls, 60 feet or more, control joints should be established every 20 feet to minimize the chances of the wall cracking because of temperature changes. These control joints are vertical breaks in the wall that allow the wall sections to move up and down but still maintain lateral rigidity. There are three types of control joints you can use, depending on what is available in your area.

One type, shaped like a rubber cross, fits into the grooved ends of special blocks. In another type, the ends of the blocks at the control joint are tongue-and-groove, one locking into the other. The third type doesn't require any special blocks, and is known as the michigan joint.

Control joints

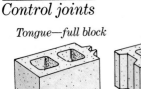

Tongue—full block

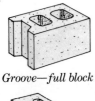

Groove—full block

Tongue—
half block

Groove—
half block

Fill control joint
with elastic caulk.

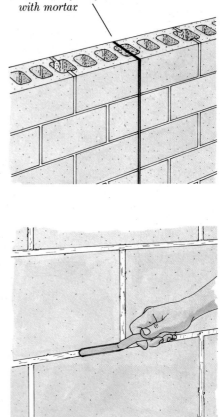

If your blocks have a cavity at
each end, as shown, fill in
each side of the felt
with mortar.

The michigan control joint is formed by slipping a piece of roofing felt or building paper between two blocks where they meet. No mortar is used on the ends of these blocks, and the paper prevents any bonding as bed mortar is squeezed up. However, you place concrete in the partial cell between the end of one block and the paper to provide lateral strength in the wall. From the illustration, you can see that alternate courses use half-blocks on each side of the joint so that it is continuous with the top of the wall.

After the wall is finished, fill the control joint with concrete caulk, which is available at hardware or masonry outlets.

Finishing Mortar Joints

As you work, keep scraping the excess mortar from the joints and reusing it by mixing it with mortar on your board. Remember that once it has hardened so it will just barely take a thumbprint, you must start tooling or striking it.

Use a convex or V-shaped jointing tool to compress all the joints. This will force some more mortar out beyond the edge of the block, which should be trimmed off with the edge of the trowel. Let the mortar dry partially, then restrike the joints to form a nice, distinct joint. Finally, brush the wall after the mortar has dried to remove any dirt or small fragments of mortar.

Finishing the joints

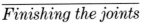

1. Compress the joints to force
out excess mortar.

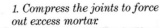

3. When mortar is almost dry,
strike it again to form even,
distinct joints.

2. Trim off excess mortar
with your trowel.

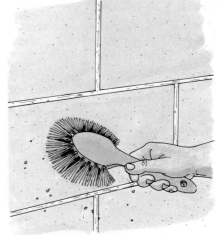

4. Finally, when the mortar is
dry, brush away any
remaining fragments
or dirt particles.

Pilasters in block walls

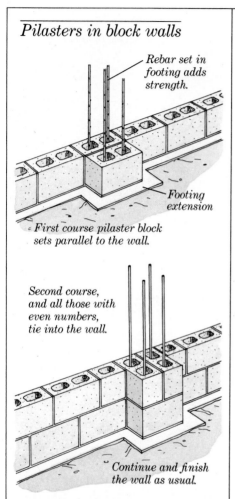

Rebar set in footing adds strength.

Footing extension

First course pilaster block sets parallel to the wall.

Second course, and all those with even numbers, tie into the wall.

Continue and finish the wall as usual.

Building Pilasters

On long, straight retaining walls, reinforcing buttresses, called pilasters, can be built into the wall for additional strength. Since these blocks must also be supported by a concrete footing, plan ahead when designing the wall and footing. Even greater strength can be achieved by filling the pilasters either with concrete or with reinforcing rods and concrete.

Capping the Wall

A garden or retaining wall of concrete block is not complete until it is capped. The cap not only gives the wall a finished appearance but also prevents moisture from entering it. The cap can be applied in several different ways.

Capping a block wall

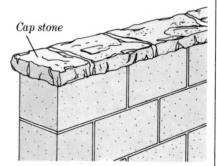

Concrete block walls are commonly capped with flat concrete blocks, which are simply mortared in place on top of the wall. In this case, leave the mortared joints flush rather than tooling them, which would cause a slight depression that catches moisture.

Cap stone

Block walls can also be capped with stone, such as flagstone, for a more decorative finish. Fill the cores of the top course of blocks with pieces of scrap block and concrete before mortaring the stone cap in place. Project the stone ¾ inch beyond the sides of the wall, so water will drip off the cap rather than enter the wall.

If the wall is to be stuccoed, as described below, one common method of capping a wall is to cover it with a rounded layer of concrete. The top course of block must first be filled with concrete. One way is to cover the top of the last course of blocks with wire mesh or roofing felt to prevent the concrete on the final course from falling through to the bottom of the wall.

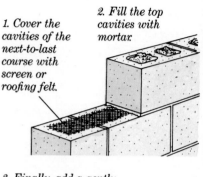

1. Cover the cavities of the next-to-last course with screen or roofing felt.

2. Fill the top cavities with mortar.

3. Finally, add a gently rounded cap of concrete.

Be sure that the mesh or felt just covers the webs and not the edges. While the mortar in the cores is still fresh, begin laying on the top layer of concrete, building it up in the center and then rounding it over the top of the wall with the trowel, much like smoothing frosting on a cake.

Covering the Blocks

If you desire, concrete block walls can be covered with a stucco finish. Stucco is similar to concrete but doesn't contain any gravel. Unlike stuccoing a house, no wire has to be stretched over the block first to hold it on the wall. If your stuccoing efforts are somewhat rough, that only adds to the rustic charm of the wall.

Before applying the stucco, paint the block wall with a concrete bonding agent that can be found in most hardware stores. Make the stucco mix of 1 part portland cement, 1 part hydrated lime, and 6 parts fine sand. You can also use one part masonry cement, which already contains the hydrated lime, and 3 parts sand. Add water until the mix has a rich, creamy texture. Stucco is applied in two separate coats: the scratch coat and the finish coat, which can be mixed with a coloring agent.

Stuccoing a block wall

1. Coat the blocks with a concrete bonding agent.

2. Apply the scratch coat with a square finishing trowel.

3. Score the scratch coat horizontally with a store-bought or homemade scarifier (see text).

4. After 48 hours, apply the finish coat with a plasterer's trowel. This coat can be colored and applied smoothly or with any texture you desire.

The scratch coat. The first coat is troweled on with a flat finishing trowel rather than a pointed trowel. Work from the top of the wall down. Press the mortar firmly against the block and smooth it out until it is just ⅜ inch thick. Before it dries, the stucco must be scored about ¼ inch deep so the second coat will bond tightly to it. Rent a special tool for this called a scarifier, or simply scratch the wall up with several pieces of wire tied together and then spread apart, something like a broom. Keep this first coat damp for 48 hours, either by repeatedly spraying it or by covering the wall with plastic that is weighted at the ends and the ground to trap the moist air.

The finish coat. Apply the second coat in the same fashion, making it also just ⅜ inch thick, but leaving it smooth when finished. This coat can be colored by adding a coloring agent to the stucco as you mix it, which eliminates the need to paint the finish coat. The coloring agent will come with complete instructions for adding it to the stucco.

Surface-Bonded Block

New on the market is a fast and inexpensive alternative to building the traditional concrete block wall. It is the surface-bonding agent, a mixture of portland cement and chopped fiberglass. Instead of mortaring each block in place one by one, the entire wall is simply stacked tightly together then coated with the bonding agent.

The fiberglass fibers interlock over the joints between the blocks and give the surface-bonding agent its great strength. Government tests show bonded block walls have six times the lateral strength of conventionally mortared walls. However, because it is so new, check with your building inspector about its acceptability in your area.

A surface-bonded wall is constructed by mortaring the first course in place on the footing. After that, stack all the concrete blocks tightly together in a running-bond pattern.

Once the wall is up, the bonding agent is applied no more than ⅛ inch thick to all sides of the wall.

Coloring agents are available for the bonding material, and the walls can be stuccoed over or painted when completed. Cap the walls in one of the standard manners described above.

Surface-bonding agents are not widely sold, but can be obtained from one of the following sources if unavailable locally:

W.R. Bonsal Company
   Box 241148
   Charlotte, NC 28224

Q-Bond Corp. of America
   Box 16493
   Denver, CO 80216

Quik Wall
   1790 Century Circle
   Atlanta, GA 30345

Stone Mountain Mfg. Company
   5750 Chesapeake Blvd.
   Norfolk, VA 23513

STONE PATIOS, WALKS, AND WALLS

*F*ew masonry projects are as attractive and long lasting as those done with stone. Beautiful stonework, done hundreds of years ago, can be seen in all parts of the world. The Incas and Aztecs built walls with massive stones that still stand. Some of the finest stonework in the world can be seen today in Japan and Korea, where stone was used extensively for construction of castles, city gates, moats, and walls. But stonework need not be the work of an ancient master to be attractive. The graceful stone walls in New England, built by early settlers clearing the rocky land, attest to its simple beauty.

The rugged texture and dark color of the stones in this wall contrast with the smooth, green plants in the garden.

WORKING WITH STONE

Stonemasonry requires great patience and a certain artistic flair in finding and fitting just the right stone. You can work at your own pace and quit the job at any stage when you have had enough for one day.

Stone fits in with virtually any style house or yard. A flagstone walk or patio around a garden or a rough stone wall along a low bank is natural in appearance and so inherently beautiful that it always blends with its surroundings.

Obtaining Stone

Quarried stone and fieldstone are the two basic types of stone. Become familiar with each type so you can choose the one that will be most appropriate for your project and your pocketbook.

Quarried stone. Quarried stone must be cut from a mountainside, which involves considerable labor and thus makes the price of quarried stone much higher than that of fieldstone. Quarried stone, which includes marble, flagstone, and slate, is generally cut and shaped at the work site, but the face of the stone is left natural.

Fieldstone. As the name implies, fieldstone is a simple rock found lying in fields or along rivers and streams. Fieldstone is divided into two classes: rubble and roughly squared. Rubble is just what the name says—a basic rock. Roughly squared stones have been worked over with a hammer and stone chisel to roughly shape them, making it easier to fit one against another.

Finding Stone

You have a choice of either buying your stone or finding your own. If you collect your own, the easiest place to look is along rivers and streams, but make sure you obtain permission to remove stones from private property.

If you are buying your stone, go to several different stone yards in the area and compare the materials they have on hand. If you are buying rubble, check that the stones are relatively flat rather than round. Compare prices and ask how much it will cost to deliver. Cut stone, such as ashlar and flagstone, will be the most expensive. Roughly squared stone will cost less, but will still be more expensive than ordinary rubble.

Estimating Volume

The amount of stone you need depends on the project and the type of stone you are using. Whatever your project, you first must calculate either the square footage for a patio or walk, or the cubic feet for a wall. To calculate square feet, simply multiply the length times the width. With that dimension, the stone yard can tell you how much material you will need.

If you are building a wall, you need to determine the volume. Do this by multiplying length times width times

Stones are full of character. Choose from smooth, round fieldstone obtained from fields or streams or from quarried stone that has been cut to shape.

height, which gives you the number of cubic feet. Masonry yards often sell rock by the cubic yard. To find how many cubic yards are in your wall, divide the cubic footage by 27.

When ordering any stone that has been cut, add 10 percent to your total to allow for breakage during the project. If you are building a wall from fieldstone, add 25 percent to your total because many of the rocks you get simply won't fit.

How to Cut Stone

Fortunately, you don't need many tools for stonework, and some of them you probably already have around the house. Here is a list of the tools that will get you through virtually any type of stonemasonry:
■ Five-pound sledge hammer to provide the necessary striking weight. Don't try to get by with an ordinary hammer—not only is it too light, but the face of the hammer may chip from repeated blows on the chisel.
■ Stonemason's chisels—one called a pitching chisel that resembles a brickset but is considerably heavier, and a pointing chisel.
■ Protective eyewear—either shatterproof glasses or preferably plastic goggles. These are essential, since many small stone chips will be striking you when you are cutting rock.

Those are the main items you need for stonemasonry, but you will also need some other common tools such as a shovel, wheelbarrow, and cement trowel when mortaring stone. A pair of heavy work gloves will save you from getting cuts and blisters. Another good idea is to always wear a shirt when cutting stone, even on a hot day, so you won't get cut by flying chips.

Stone doesn't always need to be cut, particularly if you are just building a dry stone wall, but cutting will help considerably in fitting the stones together. Cutting stones is not as difficult as you might imagine, so don't hesitate to give it a try.

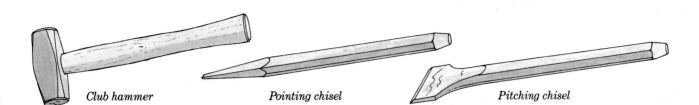

Club hammer   *Pointing chisel*   *Pitching chisel*

Cutting Fieldstone

When cutting fieldstone, place the rock to be cut on a surface that is firm but still resilient. You can put it on the ground, on a bed of sand, or on scrap pieces of wood. Do not place the stone on concrete or another large stone because the striking blows during the cutting process may cause the stone you are working on to crack in the wrong place.

Once you have decided where to cut, usually at some protrusion or sharp irregularity that you want to remove, mark a line with chalk, crayon, or a soft pencil. Score the line with moderate blows of hammer and chisel. Turn the stone over and repeat the process on the other side. Now place the chisel on the mark and strike it sharply with the hammer. After the cut is complete, dress the edge with a little more hammer and chisel work. If you see a natural fissure in the rock near the proposed cut, make your cut there since it will probably break along that line anyway. Not all rocks will crack; just put aside the ones that won't until you find a place for them.

To remove any bumps or sharp irregularities on a stone, use the pointing chisel. Simply place the point at the base of the bump, and give it a sharp rap with the hammer.

Cutting Flagstone

You will generally turn and twist and move your flagstones until you find ones that fit together naturally, but sometimes you have to cut them. Fortunately, it's not too difficult. To cut flagstone, first mark and score the line on one side with the chisel. Then place the stone over a length of pipe or some scrap 2 by 4, as illustrated, and strike sharply on the scored line with hammer and chisel. To cut a curve that matches an adjoining piece of flagstone, place the stone to be cut over the other stone and draw an outline of the curve with a pencil. Score the line and cut as described above.

With all this preparatory work finished, including having tons of rock piled in your yard, you are ready for the fun of actual construction.

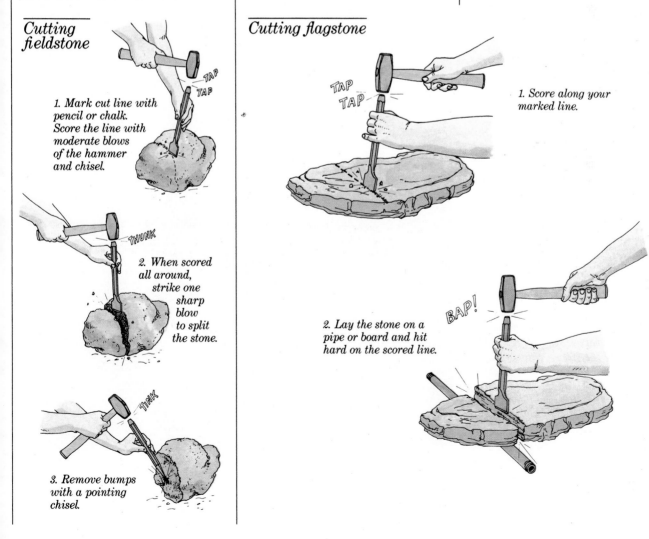

Cutting fieldstone

1. Mark cut line with pencil or chalk. Score the line with moderate blows of the hammer and chisel.

2. When scored all around, strike one sharp blow to split the stone.

3. Remove bumps with a pointing chisel.

Cutting flagstone

1. Score along your marked line.

2. Lay the stone on a pipe or board and hit hard on the scored line.

A STONE WALK

Arock walkway across your lawn or through the garden is an excellent design tactic. The natural charm of a simple stone walk can add to the relaxing mood of the garden. A stone walk is easy to build and requires few stones.

The first step is to lay out the pathway, which is done simply by laying a rope or garden hose where you want the path to be. Next, lay the stones on the grass to get a clearer picture of how it will look. The walkway can be either single stepping-stones or clusters of stones so that two people can pass. Space single stepping-stones a comfortable stride apart, not so close that you have to tiptoe, nor so far apart that you have to stretch for each one.

With the stones in place on the grass, flattest side up, use a trowel to cut the sod in the exact outline of the stone. Remove the sod, then dig the dirt out until the top of the rock is about 1 inch above the lawn surface. The stepping-stone will eventually settle. It will usually be necessary to put dirt back in the hole and pack it down until the rock sets firmly and doesn't wobble.

If you are using clusters of rocks for a wider walkway, space them about 4 or 5 inches apart so that a strip of sod remains between them, both for appearance and improved stability of the rocks.

You can use this same technique to build a patio. Such a patio is beautiful, but remember that you will have to mow the grass that grows between the stones and then sweep it clean.

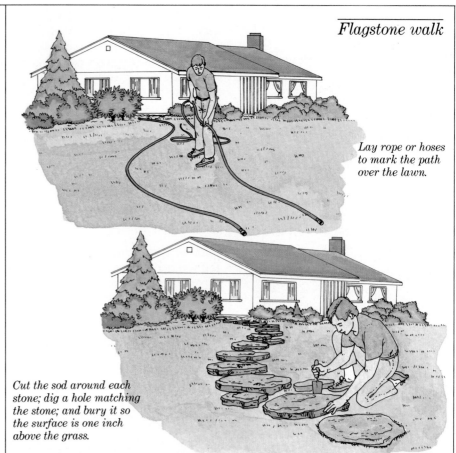

Flagstone walk

Lay rope or hoses to mark the path over the lawn.

Cut the sod around each stone; dig a hole matching the stone; and bury it so the surface is one inch above the grass.

This casual stone walk gives visitors the feeling of a relaxing walk through the woods.

A FLAGSTONE PATIO

Flagstone is a natural for constructing a patio. It's attractive, durable, and surprisingly easy to work with. Flagstone can be found naturally in many parts of the country, but more likely you will end up buying it.

Construction Techniques

One simple method for building a flagstone patio is to place each flagstone individually in a lawn, as in the stone walkway on page 56. Press the stones into the soil until they don't rock, then plant the intervening spaces with grass seed.

The best flagstone patios, however, are laid in a bed of mortar on a concrete slab.

As you can see, this involves a lot of concrete and mortar work. But if you already have a slab in the back yard that bores you, here's a way to refurbish it. If you don't already have a slab or sidewalk waiting to be covered with flagstone, see pages 70–77 for construction details.

The varied shapes and colors of flagstone make it a good choice for a large patio.

Before using mortar, lay the flagstones out so you can see how they fit. Spend some time rearranging them to minimize the number to be cut. This also lets you see whether you have enough stone on hand.

Mixing Mortar

Now mix your mortar, using 1 part portland cement to 3 parts masonry sand. Keep the mix fairly stiff so it will support the flagstones. Make sure the stones have been brushed clean.

Laying Flagstone

When you're ready to place the stones in mortar, spread on the slab a bed of mortar about 1 inch thick, or more if necessary to firmly seat 2 or 3 stones. Rap each stone firmly with the handle of the trowel to make sure it is seated.

Space the stones approximately ½ inch from one another and from the edging. You will have to turn the stones to fit them together as best you can, something like putting a jigsaw puzzle together. Because of their irregular surfaces, it is impossible to set the stones perfectly level, but you can come close by laying a straight 2 by 4 across several stones at a time with a level on top to check your work. If one stone is too high, press it further into the mortar. If a stone is too low, take it out and add mortar, then fit it back in place.

As you work your way toward the center, put down a large piece of ½-inch plywood to distribute your weight evenly on the flagstones. When all stones have been placed, let the mortar set at least 24 hours before you begin filling the joints. Fill the joints by carefully troweling in wet mortar so as little as possible falls on the flagstone. If any mortar falls on the stones, wipe it up immediately with a large, wet sponge that you rinse in a nearby bucket of water. As you work, pack the mortar firmly in the joints, and then smooth it with a slicker tool or with your trowel.

Curing the Mortar

For the mortar to cure properly, it should not dry out too rapidly. The best curing method is to cover the entire patio with sheets of plastic weighted at the edges and at all joints. This traps the moisture and allows the mortar to cure slowly, which greatly increases its strength. If you don't have plastic, you can periodically spray the patio to keep it wet, but in hot weather this can mean hosing it down every hour. Let it cure for about four days before allowing any heavy traffic on it.

Flagstone patio

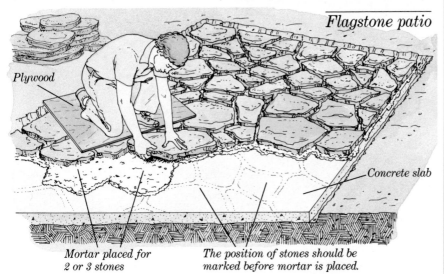

Plywood

Concrete slab

Mortar placed for 2 or 3 stones

The position of stones should be marked before mortar is placed.

A STONE WALL

If your yard has not been landscaped, and numerous rocks are lying about, put them to good use. Build a stone wall. You will not only clear the land but also gain an attractive freestanding or retaining wall.

You can build a stone wall with or without mortar depending on the desired appearance and strength. Mortared stone walls require considerably more work, since you will be dealing with sizable amounts of mortar. A mortared stone wall is not only more permanent than a dry-laid wall but appears more finished.

The height of your wall may be regulated by your local building codes. Generally, you are free to build a wall 3 feet or shorter in height without a permit. Higher walls may require a permit and possibly even an engineering study, so check with your building inspector first.

Building a Mortared Stone Wall

A mortared stone wall is a showpiece in any yard or garden, and is certain to elicit favorable comments from all guests. Constructing such a wall requires considerably more work than a dry-laid wall, but if you have the patience and time, you will be pleased with your effort.

Construction Preparations

A mortared wall, unlike a dry-laid wall, is inflexible and thus must be supported by a solid footing. Without a footing, a mortared wall may crack due to settling or frost heave. To prepare the footing ditch, first lay out the wall site with stakes and string.

The footing should be 6 inches wider than the base of the wall and at least 6 inches thick. In addition, it should have two lengths of ½-inch reinforcing rod placed in the middle to prevent the footing from cracking. In areas where the ground doesn't freeze in winter, dig the footing ditch 8 inches deep, so that the top of the footing will be 2 inches below the ground level. In cold climates, dig the footing ditch below the frost level. For specific details on how to pour and level this footing, see the section on concrete footings on page 68. Allow the footing to harden for two days before starting the actual wall.

It is a good idea to install drainage holes that allow water to escape from behind the wall. Install these drains as described for brick walls on page 39.

The flagstone cap adds to the finished look of this mortared stone wall and keeps water from seeping into the mortar joints.

Mortar Mix

The mortar used to lay a stone wall is similar to that used for a brick wall but, to support the heavy rocks, it must be made a little stiffer by using a little less water. Also, you should use some hydrated lime, which makes the mortar bind better and reduces the staining of mortar on the stones. A standard mortar mix is 1 part portland cement, 1 part hydrated lime, and 6 parts sand. Mix mortar as described for laying bricks, page 33. Add enough water to wet the mortar mix, but it should not be creamy, like brick mortar. When you trowel on stone mortar, it should stay in place, not ooze down the side of a rock.

Applying Mortar

One important step to remember before you apply mortar to any stones is to clean the rocks of any dirt or sand that would prevent the mortar from bonding to the stone. Either brush the rocks or wash with a hard stream of water.

Place a couple of shovelfuls of mortar on a piece of plywood on the ground beside you, instead of working from the wheelbarrow. Don't be too delicate when placing the mortar, but instead throw it from the trowel on to the rock. Work the mortar with the tip of the trowel to settle it into the opening, then put the stone in place. Rap the stone firmly with the end of the trowel handle to settle it and force out any air bubbles. Scrape off any excess mortar and throw the scrapings into the center part of the wall.

Mortar will begin to set in about 30 minutes, so don't spread too much at once. If the mortar in the wheelbarrow gets too stiff while you are getting started, add a little water.

To keep the stones clean as you work, have a pail of water with a large sponge handy to wipe off spills immediately.

Fitting the Stones

The key to building a good wall is to carefully select and fit each stone. The only way to do this properly is to dry-fit each stone before applying mortar. Never fit an awkward rock with the idea that the mortar alone will keep it from falling out. Gravity will eventually win this battle.

Laying the first course. Start the first course by laying out the largest stones on the footing, turning them back and forth to get a smooth and stable fit. Now remove the stones, spread a 2-inch-thick layer of mortar on the footing, and set the rocks in place. Keep in mind that you are building a wall that is two wythes wide, with the center portion filled with small rubble and mortar. The motto for a good stonemason is "One rock over two, two rocks over one."

This will help you avoid aligning joints directly over one another, which weakens the wall.

Building the ends. After you have set the first course in mortar, start building up the ends. Stretch mason's twine or nylon cord between two stakes driven at each end of the wall and set the twine or cord about 3 or 4 inches above the top of the next course. Use this as a rough guide to keep your wall level. Use the flattest stones with the smoothest faces for the end wall construction. Interlock the stones as much as possible. With the two ends built up, start laying courses in the middle section.

Mortared wall

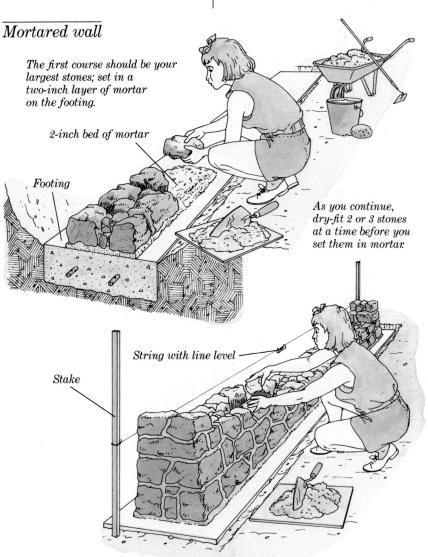

The first course should be your largest stones; set in a two-inch layer of mortar on the footing.

2-inch bed of mortar

Footing

As you continue, dry-fit 2 or 3 stones at a time before you set them in mortar.

String with line level

Stake

Mortared wall

Don't be delicate in placing mortar—throw it from trowel to rock, then work it in with the tip of the trowel.

Place bond stones every 4 feet or so about halfway up the wall.

Bond stones

Cap stone

A row of flat bond stones make the best cap stones for your wall.

Laying the middle courses. Dry-fit several stones at a time, then remove them, apply the mortar, and fit them back into place. When fitting stones against each other, spread mortar on the one already in place.

As you work your way up, remember to lay bond stones across the wall to tie it together. Place these about 4 feet apart horizontally, and approximately in the middle of the wall, or more often if you have good bond stones. Don't try to raise the wall more than about two courses in a day, or the additional weight will force mortar out of the lower joints.

Capping the wall. A beautiful way to finish a wall is to cap it with a row of flat bond stones, but it is not often that you have enough for this. Instead, mortar the flattest stones you have in place along the top of the wall. Do not rake the top joints, as described below, but leave them flush with the top edges of the stone for a more finished look.

Jointing a Stone Wall

The mortar in the face joints of a stone wall can be either left flush with the rocks or raked out. Many people prefer to rake the joints because the shadows over the indentations add definition to the wall. You can remove up to 1½ inches of mortar in the joints without weakening the wall. This is most easily done with the end of an old broom handle or a piece of ¾-inch pipe.

When you rake the joints is important, since the mortar should be neither too hard nor too soft. The mortar has set the proper time for jointing when you can just leave a shallow thumbprint in the mortar when pressing it firmly. This is about half an hour after the mortar has been applied, so if you are building a long wall, be careful that you joint the first part before the mortar has set too hard.

Rake the joints to the depth that suits you best, then go over them with a soft brush, such as an old paint brush, to clear away the excess mortar. For a smoother joint, go over them again with a jointing tool.

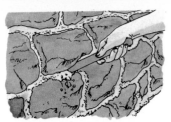

1. Rake mortar from joints with a piece of broom handle.

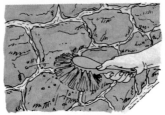

2. Brush away crumbs of excess mortar.

3. Finish by smoothing the joints with a jointing tool.

A Dry Stone Wall

Stone walls can be laid straight or curved, with vertical sides or battered, meaning tapered back at the top. Unless you have a lot of flat rocks, your walls should be battered for greater stability. Make a batter gauge from 1 by 2 lumber, or from any scrap wood, to guide your work. The rule of thumb for battering a wall is to tilt it back 1 inch for every 2 feet of rise.

In constructing a freestanding dry wall, there is a correlation between height and thickness. The rule of thumb here is that a wall 3 feet high should be 2 feet wide at the base. For every 6 inches you raise the wall beyond that, widen the base 4 inches. However, if you are building a low retaining wall, only 2 or 3 feet high, against an existing bank, the wall need only be one stone thick. In such a case, it is a good idea to first batter the dirt bank with a pick and shovel before building the wall.

Constructing the Wall

A dry stone wall is built much like a wet stone wall (page 58) except there is no mortar. This process takes patience because you do not just stack stones, you carefully select each stone for the best fit. If a stone is not well anchored in place, it will eventually fall out and part of the wall will collapse. A stone wall is built by laying two parallel wythes of stone with small rubble filling in the center. As the wall goes up, long and flat bond stones must be placed periodically across the wall to tie the two wythes together.

Whether or not you need a footing to support the wall depends on your winter climate. If the ground freezes, you should dig a footing ditch below the frost line and place your largest stones there as a footing. Otherwise, frost heave will likely topple part of your wall every winter. You can also pour a concrete footing, as described for a mortared stone wall on page 58.

Laying the base. To start the wall, first lay out the largest and flattest stones for the base. Mark the perimeter of the wall, then excavate it about 4 inches deep, or below the frost line in cold areas. Place the stones on the ground in the footing ditch and make sure they do not wobble. Dig out dirt or pack some in below this base course to stabilize them. Make sure that the stones in this base course do not tilt out, since this will make successive courses tilt away from each other, resulting in a weak wall.

Building the ends. The most challenging part of good wall construction is building the ends or right-angle corners. It is a common practice to build the ends or corners first, then fill in the center section of the wall. Use your longest and flattest rocks for the ends and corners. From the illustration, you can see how the stones are placed so that each one interlocks with the others. Select the rocks with the smoothest faces to give the wall a finished appearance. Take

your time here because good construction at this point is important to the stability of the entire wall. If you can't find rocks that fit well enough, try cutting some. The wall is going to be around for many years, and you want it to look right.

Laying the other courses. Lay each course of stone as described for the wet stone wall, using the guide string to show you where to raise or lower wall sections. Check the face of the wall periodically with the batter guide and level.

Remember to tie the wall together with bond stones placed about every 4 feet measured horizontally when the wall is about half complete.

Capping the wall. Lay a series of flat bond stones across the top, not only to give it a finished appearance but to hold the wall firmly together. If you have a lot of irregularly shaped rocks left over, fit them along the top of the wall. You can greatly increase the strength of the wall if you mortar this last course in place as shown for a wet wall on page 60.

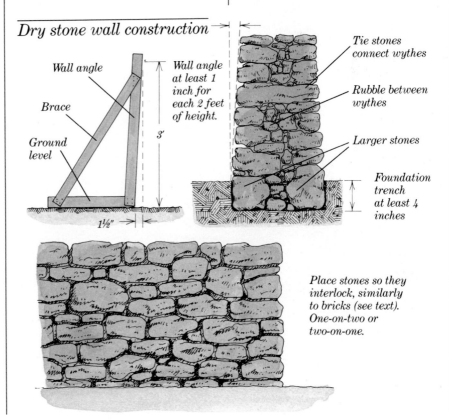

Dry stone wall construction

Wall angle

Brace

Ground level

Wall angle at least 1 inch for each 2 feet of height.

3'

1½"

Tie stones connect wythes

Rubble between wythes

Larger stones

Foundation trench at least 4 inches

Place stones so they interlock, similarly to bricks (see text). One-on-two or two-on-one.

CONCRETE IN THE LANDSCAPE

*C*oncrete can be used around your landscape in numerous ways, ranging from a footing for a brick wall to an exposed aggregate patio covered with beautiful stone. Concrete can be shaped, colored, and finished in so many different fashions it is sometimes difficult to tell it is concrete. This liquid stone is one of the most versatile of all building materials, and you can take advantage of its strength and adaptability in planning both your garden and your yard.

Many concrete projects are within the realm of the do-it-yourselfer, so don't hesitate to consider a concrete project even if you have never worked with concrete before.

This concrete walk features curved edges, an aggregate surface, and some steps to create an interesting focal point in this desert landscape.

WORKING WITH CONCRETE

You may want to use concrete for a patio, walkway, driveway, or the footings for a wall. Whatever the projects, they should all be planned together so they will integrate with one another, not clash.

Concrete is very permanent, so make sure you use graph paper as described in Chapter 2 to carefully plan each project before you actually start. You can imagine how much easier it is to erase a concrete walkway on graph paper than it would be to remove an actual one from your landscape. However, if you don't like any of your existing concrete walks or your patio, they can be removed by breaking them up with a rented jackhammer.

The Recipe

One of the first things to keep in mind is the difference between cement, concrete, and mortar. Concrete is made by mixing specific amounts of cement, sand, gravel, and water. Mortar is a mixture of cement, sand, and water—no gravel.

The most common type of cement is portland cement, named after the gray stone on England's Isle of Portland. Cement is a dry powder mixture of lime, clay, and gypsum that is ground so finely that it will pass through a screen with 40,000 openings to the square inch. When it is mixed with water, a chemical reaction occurs that causes it to harden.

Aggregates and Water

The sand and gravel that are added to a concrete mix are known as aggregates, and they make up about 70 percent of the mix. Sand, which is either natural or made by crushing rocks, is considered a fine aggregate.

Gravel, or sometimes crushed stone, is a coarse aggregate. It ranges in size from ¼ inch to 1½ inches in diameter. As a general rule, most projects call for medium-sized gravel, which is ¾ inch. At any rate, the diameter of gravel should not be more than one third of the thickness of the concrete slab.

When mixing in aggregates, it is important that they be free of dirt, which prevents the cement from bonding to the gravel and weakens the mix. Store aggregates on sheets of plastic or plywood; this not only keeps them clean but also keeps the material from being wasted.

Water, the catalyst that causes the cement to harden and bind to the aggregates, should be clean enough to drink. How much water you add will vary slightly with the purpose of the concrete. The less water used, the stronger the mix, but less water will also make the concrete stiffer and more difficult to work with. The amount of water is also related to how wet your sand is. Sand sold in bulk is usually always wet. Different amounts of water are specified, such as 6 gallons of water for each sack of cement when the sand is damp, or 5½ gallons when the sand is wet. But in actual practice, no one mixes concrete that way; instead, they add specific mixes of cement and aggregates together, then add enough water to make a thick, creamy mix.

Calculating Volume

Your concrete needs are always figured in yards, meaning cubic yards. To calculate your needs, use this formula: Thickness (in inches) times length (in feet) times width (in feet), divided by 12 gives you the number of cubic feet. Divide that by 27 to get the number of cubic yards. Use the charts on the facing page for a ready reference on calculating volume.

Calculating volume sounds simple enough on paper, but when ordering concrete in a transit-mix truck, you had better do it carefully, since too little or too much will cost you money.

This concrete patio requires little maintenance and provides a nonslip surface around the pool.

Calculating Concrete Areas

Determine the patio area in square feet and thickness in inches. For rectangles, multiply width by length; for circles, 3.14 times the radius squared. Draw complex shapes on graph paper, each square equal to one square foot. Count all squares more than half within the shape.

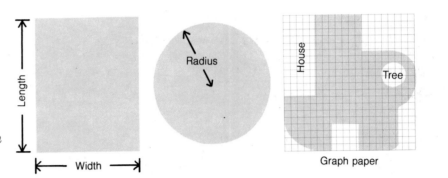

Width

Length

Radius

House

Tree

Graph paper

Calculating Volume of Concrete

Find the point where a vertical line from the number of square feet you have crosses the red line for the thickness you want. From there, follow a horizontal line to the scale at the right to find the amount of concrete you will need.

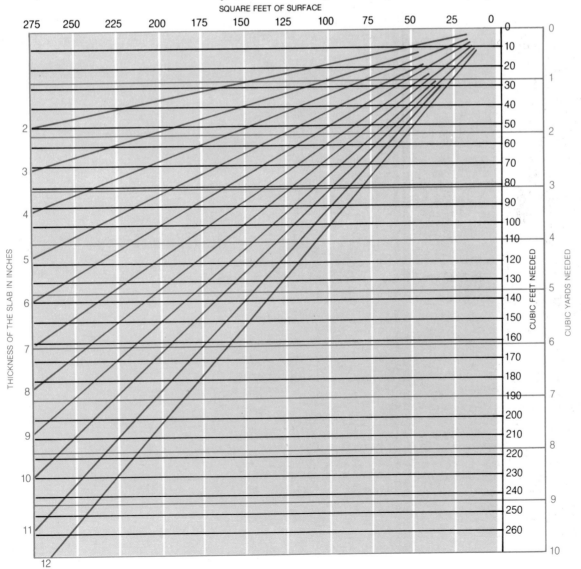

When you have footing trenches, get in the trenches and measure them. When building a slab, don't forget to calculate the footing trench around the perimeter.

After you have doublechecked your volume estimate, add 10 percent to the actual order. Ordering 10 percent extra is vastly cheaper than bringing the truck back for half a yard to finish the job. If you do have a little left over, have some other small concrete jobs ready, such as some forms for concrete stepping-stones.

If you are mixing your own concrete, keep in mind that portland cement is sold in 94-pound sacks that equal 1 cubic foot. You will need 5 sacks of cement for each yard of concrete in a standard mix, or 6 sacks in a richer mix.

Calculate sand and gravel needs according to how many yards of concrete you will require. For instance, if your slab calls for 8 yards of concrete, order 8 yards of sand and 8 of gravel (remember to add about 10 percent to all your orders to make sure you have enough).

For small jobs, you can buy a sack of premixed concrete; you only add the water. One such sack holds ⅔ cubic foot.

Tools

Working with concrete requires the use of some tools you probably have on hand, plus some which may be new and unfamiliar. Many of the new tools have interesting names, such as bull float and darby, and are used to smooth the surface of the concrete. The tools you will need are shown at the tops of the pages in each section where their use is described.

Mixing Concrete

Concrete can be mixed on a sheet of plywood for small jobs, or for larger jobs in a wheelbarrow or concrete mixer. For even larger jobs, the easiest way is to have it delivered in a transit-mix truck.

Mixing concrete

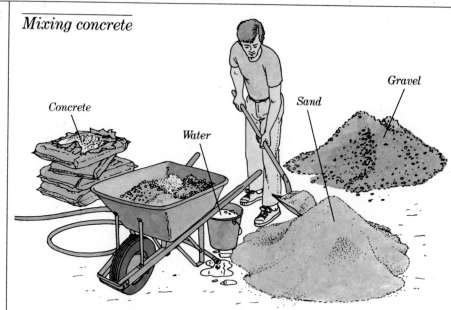

Concrete   Water   Sand   Gravel

By the Wheelbarrow

There is no mystery to mixing concrete, even though there are many different formulas. You won't go wrong if you use either one of the two given here. For footings and edgings, use 1 part cement, 3 parts sand, and 4 parts gravel. Where you need greater strength, such as in driveways or slabs, increase the amount of cement by reducing the amount of sand. This stronger mix should be made of 1 part cement, 2 to 2¼ parts sand, and 3 parts gravel.

Whether you are mixing the ingredients in a wheelbarrow or portable mixer, it is done the same way—by the shovelful. Just be careful that you keep your shovel loads equal. You can put about twice as much wet sand on a shovel as you can dry cement. When mixing by hand, put the sand and cement in the wheelbarrow and mix them together, then add the gravel and mix again. Finally, add the water. On your first attempt at mixing, you will probably add too much water. This is a common mistake. In this case, add some more cement and aggregates in proper proportion and mix until your concrete is a uniform color.

By the Truckload

Some projects, like a sidewalk or patio that is divided up into sections, you can do by mixing your own concrete; others, like a large slab for a garage, usually require the use of a transit-mix concrete truck. One thing about ordering concrete from a truck—you need several helpers around. The concrete comes fast and you are allowed only a few minutes of free time for each yard delivered; after that you are charged by the minute. Typically, you are allowed five free minutes to place each yard of concrete.

Placing the order. When ordering concrete, you are likely to be asked first how many yards you want. Then you will be asked whether you want a 5-sack mix or a 6-sack mix, meaning 5 or 6 sacks of cement used in each yard of mix. Order 5-sack mix for footings, edgings, and perimeter foundations, and order the stronger 6-sack mix for slabs such as walks, patios, and driveways. In most cases, the firm's dispatcher will be able to offer good advice on what type of concrete mix you should have, depending on the job. Feel free to ask questions, and if you don't get satisfactory answers, call another transit-mix firm.

Pumpers. Sometimes a truck will not be able to reach your work site because it is too steep, too wooded, or too muddy. In such a case, you must order a pumper, either on your own or through the transit-mix company. Pumpers cost $100 to $200 for a pour, which sounds expensive but may make the difference between doing the job or not. In addition, a pumper is faster than a truck, and can thus cut your costs. When using a pumper, the concrete truck will back up to the pumper and pour the concrete into it. The concrete is then pumped through a 4-inch or 5-inch-diameter hose to your project site. The size hose called for will depend on the size aggregate you are using. If a pumper is required, explain this to the transit-mix firm and to the pumper firm, since you generally will have to use somewhat smaller aggregate. They will tell you what size aggregate to use. Again, have plenty of help on hand when the pour starts. It normally takes two people to handle the pumper hose, one to direct it and another to support the hose as it is moved about the site.

Additives. When working in abnormally cold or hot weather, some additives may have to be added to the concrete mix. These should be discussed with the dispatcher when placing an order.

One additive used in areas with severe freezing is an agent that causes millions of tiny air bubbles to be trapped in the concrete. This is called an air-entraining agent. The air bubbles may weaken the concrete a bit, but they prevent it from cracking when it contracts or expands with the weather. When mixing your own concrete, you must have a concrete mixer to make air-entrained concrete; mixing the agent into the concrete by shovel in a wheelbarrow is too slow for it to form the bubbles.

Another agent commonly used in severe cold areas is calcium chloride, which makes the concrete set more quickly than normal. This helps prevent the water in the concrete from freezing and expanding, which can fracture the pour.

When working in weather hotter than 90 degrees, you may need to keep the concrete from setting too fast. Here you add a set-retarding agent. Again, the dispatcher can advise you, depending on the weather and their own experience in the area.

The fourth type of additive sometimes used is a plasticizer, which reduces the amount of water in the mix, helping prevent such problems as excessive shrinkage and cracking.

Now that you are familiar with mixes, tools, and ordering, you are ready to start some projects. One of the easiest is pouring a footing for a masonry wall. After the section on wall footings, you will learn to pour a lawn edging with forms, then to pour a slab such as a driveway, patio, or sidewalk. The different finishing techniques for smoothing the surface of the concrete will be covered in this last section. These include techniques for making patterns in the concrete as well as adding color.

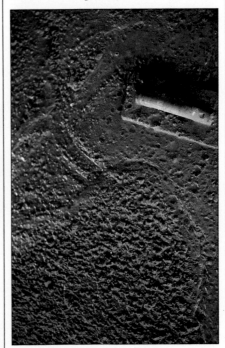

After the concrete is poured, finish it to the desired smoothness with a tool, such as this wood float.

Rent a pumper for areas where the concrete truck can't get close enough to the pour site.

WALL FOOTING

T*he simplest way to pour a footing for a brick or stone wall is to use the footing ditch as a form for the concrete. The trick here is to make the surface of the concrete level when the ground is bound to be irregular. You do this with leveling stakes, as described below.*

The footing for a wall is generally 2 or 3 inches below the ground surface, so that no concrete is visible around the wall. The footing should be twice the width of the wall and at least 6 inches thick. It may have to be thicker if it must be placed below the frost line, or freezing level, of the ground. The addition of ⅜-inch reinforcing rods (rerods) placed in the footing will markedly strengthen it. You can either pour half the thickness of the footing and then put the rerod in place, or tie the rerod to the leveling stakes and pour all at once.

Dig the footings to the required depth and width. Use a square-nosed shovel to keep the sides and bottom of the ditch neat.

To make sure that the top of the poured footing is level, drive 2 by 2 leveling stakes in the center of the ditch every 4 feet. Drive the first stake at the low end of the footing ditch until the top is about 2 inches below the ground level. Move 4 feet down the ditch and drive the next stake. Use a 4-foot level to check that it is the same height as the other stake. There's a little trick to keeping the stakes the same height: Since the bubble is not exact, turn your level end for end on each stake to see if the bubble still appears centered.

When the stakes have been driven, pour the concrete just to the tops. With a shovel or extra stakes, poke and stir the concrete to settle it. Add a little more if necessary to bring the concrete to the top of the stakes, then smooth with a trowel. Leave the stakes in place. They will eventually rot away, but will not significantly weaken the footing. Let the footing harden for 24 hours before starting wall construction on it.

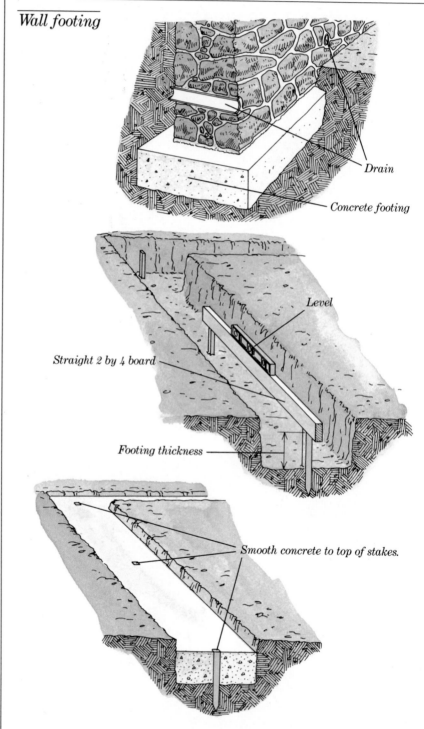

Wall footing

Drain

Concrete footing

Straight 2 by 4 board

Level

Footing thickness

Smooth concrete to top of stakes.

CONCRETE EDGING

Concrete edging serves many purposes. It provides a rigid perimeter to hold a brick-on-sand patio or walkway in place, or it can be used as lawn edging, or to separate lawn from a flower garden.

Edgings are usually set flush with the ground, particularly next to a lawn, to avoid having to hand trim the grass.

Concrete edgings are best made with forms. Curved edging forms can be made from ¼-inch plywood cut to proper dimensions, redwood bender boards, or a product on the market made from wood and plastic that is flexible and used for lawn edging.

Lawn-edging forms must be set in a ditch dug in the ground. The edging can be as wide or as narrow as you like, but if you are going to cap it with bricks, as described here, space the edging forms one brick length apart. Lay the site out first with a string stretched between two stakes to mark the outside of the edging, and another set of stakes and string exactly parallel to the first to mark the inside edge. Lay out any curves with a garden hose.

Start your digging outside the string lines, and make the ditch wide enough for you to work comfortably at setting your forms in place. Any excess room on the outside will be filled in with soil or sod. Set 1 by 6 form boards flush with the top of the finish grade, whether it be lawn, sidewalk, or patio. Use a level to make sure the tops of the forms remain level, then nail the forms to 1 by 2 stakes placed every 12 inches outside the forms. Drive the stakes down below the top of the forms or cut the tops off. Check that the spacing between the inner and outer forms is consistently just the length of a brick.

Now pour concrete in the forms, bringing it to about 2½ inches from the top of the form, which is the thickness of a brick. Work the concrete a few times with a trowel to remove any air pockets and to settle the larger pieces of aggregate. Now use the screed to smooth and level the concrete.

As soon as the sheen of water on top of the concrete has disappeared, begin placing your brick edging in the concrete. Rap each brick lightly with a rubber mallet to set it in the concrete. You can either place the bricks tightly together or space them so you can add mortared joints later, depending on how you are placing bricks in the rest of the project.

Stepping-Stones

Concrete stepping-stones resembling natural rocks make a good first project for the concrete novice. They can easily be made by digging 4-inch-deep holes in the ground in the desired shape, then filling them with concrete. Float the top as discussed for a sidewalk and press in leaves or other objects for designs, or use smooth, attractive stones for an exposed-aggregate surface.

Concrete edging

Stake the forms in place and pour concrete to about 2½ inches from the top of the forms.

Lay bricks on top of the wet concrete and tap them in place with a rubber mallet.

PATIOS AND SIDEWALKS

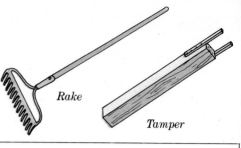

Rake

Tamper

Explaining how to pour both patios and sidewalks all at once may seem like a big order, but they are similar in many ways. A sidewalk is easier than a patio because it is smaller in scale, but the principle is the same.

So if you can do a sidewalk, you can tackle a patio. It's just bigger. In either case, the first job, called laying out the site, is to determine exactly where the sidewalk or patio will be located.

Laying Out the Site

Unlike many concrete projects—particularly foundation work—sidewalks and patios do not need to be laid out with exacting precision because nothing will be constructed on top of them. They should be laid out carefully and symmetrically, but you needn't spend a whole day carefully aligning each angle.

Sidewalks can be laid out simply by stretching two parallel strings between stakes driven into the ground. How wide should a walk be? City sidewalks are usually 5 feet wide, which is more than you are likely to need. Two people can walk comfortably together on a walk 4 feet wide, or they can pass each other on one 3 feet wide.

Working with a pick and shovel first on the outside edge of the string line, to give yourself room to set your forms, excavate the ground approximately 4 inches deep, if you want the surface of the walk to be flush with the top of the ground. Remove the string lines and remove the dirt from the interior. Level the excavated area with a square-nosed shovel and tamp it until firm, if necessary.

Building a concrete walk

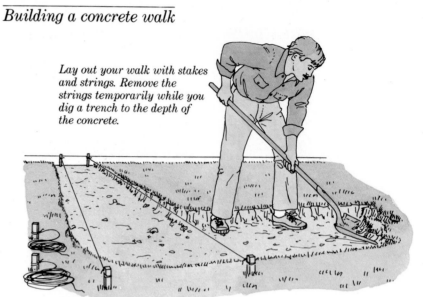

Lay out your walk with stakes and strings. Remove the strings temporarily while you dig a trench to the depth of the concrete.

Lay out a patio in the same fashion, but make any corners square by using the 3-4-5 measuring method described on page 36. Remember that there is no rule that says a patio must be square; indeed, it will be much more interesting if you add some curves or angles.

Installing the Forms

Patios and sidewalks are normally formed with 2 by 4s, which will provide a layer of concrete 3½ inches thick. In areas with severe winters, you may have to excavate deeper and place your walk or patio on gravel as explained below. Check your local codes in such cases. When making curves with forms that will be removed later, use pieces of ¼-inch plywood or doubled strips of redwood bender board staked every 6 inches on the outside for support. If the forms will remain permanently in place, make curved forms by cutting halfway through the 2 by 4 with a circular saw. Space the cuts ½ inch apart.

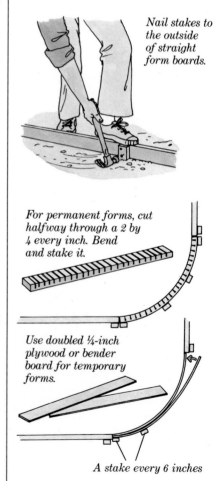

Nail stakes to the outside of straight form boards.

For permanent forms, cut halfway through a 2 by 4 every inch. Bend and stake it.

Use doubled ¼-inch plywood or bender board for temporary forms.

A stake every 6 inches

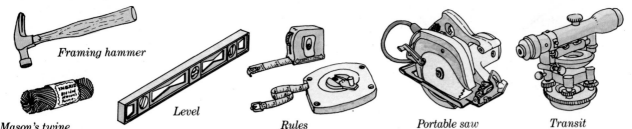

Framing hammer

Mason's twine

Level

Rules

Portable saw

Transit

Concrete walk forms

Use the head of a sledge hammer to back the nailing of bender-board or half-sawn 2 by 4 boards to make curves in the forms.

Use your level often to check the forms. If the level won't reach across set it on a straight 2 by 4 board.

Form boards for a stepped walk on sloping ground

To install the forms, first replace your string lines. The inside edges of the forms should be directly under the strings. Drive 2 by 4 stakes into the ground every 3 feet on the outside of the forms, and nail the stakes to the form boards with scaffold nails that can be pulled easily when the forms are removed. If the forms are permanent, use 16-penny (16d) nails. Wherever two form boards meet, drive a support stake at the joint. Always nail the support stakes to the form boards from the outside.

Use a level to keep the 2 by 4s level along each form. Check also that the sides are level with one another by placing a level across the forms. In the case of a wide patio, use a long, straight 2 by 4 with a level on top of it.

When building a sidewalk on irregular ground, you can raise or lower the form boards to roughly follow the contour of the ground. The most a sidewalk should ever slope is 1 inch per foot. You can also "step" a sloped walk. The steps are formed simply by placing one or two 2 by 4s across the walk, even with the top of the support stakes, and then continuing the form boards from the bottom of the crosspiece to the next step. Make the steps equidistant so you will not have to adjust your stride as you walk on them.

Sloping a Patio
Any patio next to a house should be slightly sloped so rainwater drains away from the house. A slope of 1 inch for each 10 feet will be sufficient. There are two ways to determine the slope while building the forms. The easiest way is with a transit (see page 81). With the transit method you lay out the forms closest to the house, then use the transit to determine the height of the forms farthest from the house, dropping 1 inch for every 10 feet of patio width.

Instead of using a transit, you can do a fine job with a level. Lay out the form closest to the house, keeping it level. To lay out the two side forms with a proper slope away from the house, keep the forms just a half-bubble off of level. While not as accurate as a transit, this is a quick and effective means of keeping a consistent slope to patio forms.

When forming a large patio, your work will be simplified by dividing the patio into sections with permanent forms. You can pour and finish one section at a time rather than having to do the whole patio at once.

Construction wheelbarrow

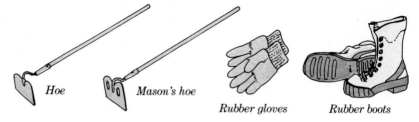

Hoe *Mason's hoe* *Rubber gloves* *Rubber boots*

The divider forms break up the plain expanse of concrete and allow the concrete to expand and contract, markedly reducing chances that the concrete will crack.

Form the divider squares with redwood or other wood impervious to weathering and contact with the ground. No square should be greater than 10 feet by 10 feet. Level and stake the long divider forms across the patio excavation area first, then nail the shorter divider forms at regular intervals. Support stakes must be driven 1 inch below the top of the forms, or cut off. Do not put a nail through the top of any forms, but instead toenail one form to another.

To prevent staining, cover the tops of the forms with masking tape before pouring concrete. You can remove the tape after the concrete has set.

Some Precautions

To avoid frost heave in areas with severe winters, your patio must be placed on a bed of gravel, and the perimeter should also be reinforced to prevent cracking. This is best done by digging a 6-inch-wide ditch around the patio perimeter that is slightly below the frost line in your area. Fill the ditch half full with gravel, then place lengths of ⅜-inch reinforcing rod around the perimeter ditch. Support the reinforcing rod on rocks so it will be in the middle of the concrete when the pour begins.

If the ground is dry, it is also a good idea to place plastic sheeting in the bottom of the form before pouring the concrete. The plastic sheeting will prevent premature drying of the concrete. Although not generally required, it is also advisable to put reinforcing wire with a 6-inch mesh between the forms for either a patio or sidewalk. The wire mesh will help notably in preventing the concrete from cracking due to slight settling or shifting. Support it on small rocks so it will be in the center of the concrete when the pour is complete.

Concrete paving forms

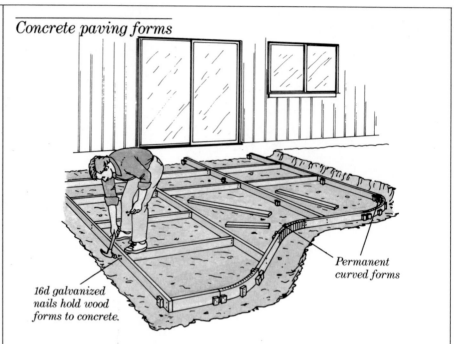

16d galvanized nails hold wood forms to concrete.

Permanent curved forms

Pouring the Concrete

When mixing and pouring your own concrete, remember that you are pouring only one wheelbarrowful at a time. If you are pouring a patio that is divided into 10-foot by 10-foot sections, or a sidewalk divided into much smaller sections, one wheelbarrow load will not go far. In such cases, spread the concrete as evenly as possible across the section you are pouring. Then, with your next wheelbarrowful, add another even layer on top of the first. Keep working your way up in this manner until you can pour and finish the top layer all at once. Don't pour a section piece by piece because it will be hardened and irregular before you finish.

Whether you are pouring the concrete yourself or hiring a transit-mix truck, remember to work the concrete with a shovel or stake to break up any air pockets. Use a rented jitterbug tamper to settle the gravel below the surface. Do not overwork the mix, however, or you will cause the aggregates to separate, which weakens the concrete. Tamp just enough to settle the coarse aggregates below the surface.

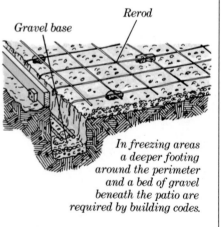

Rerod

Gravel base

In freezing areas a deeper footing around the perimeter and a bed of gravel beneath the patio are required by building codes.

If you are making a pour from a transit-mix truck, you or a friend experienced with concrete work will have to handle the chute. Your job is to keep the chute moving along the forms until just enough concrete has been placed. There is no gate in the chute to stop the concrete; it only stops when the operator stops pumping concrete into the chute. You should agree in advance with the truck operator on a few hand signals.

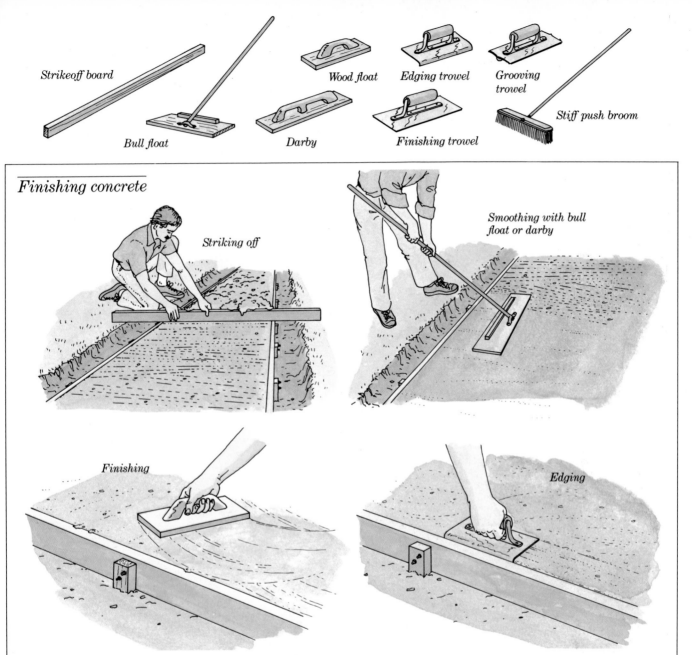

Strikeoff board

Bull float

Wood float

Darby

Edging trowel

Finishing trowel

Grooving trowel

Stiff push broom

Finishing concrete

Striking off

Smoothing with bull float or darby

Finishing

Edging

Finishing Concrete

Even as concrete is being placed in forms, helpers should be starting the numerous steps that go into finishing concrete. These steps include striking off the concrete, floating it, rounding the edges and placing control joints, then giving it the final floating.

Striking off. Once the concrete has been worked, it should be leveled with the top of the forms, a process known as striking off or screeding the concrete. This is done by placing a straight 2 by 4 across the forms, then working it forward, never backward, using a zig-zag sawing motion to level the concrete. If there are humps or depressions in the concrete after your first pass, go over it again. You may need to throw in a shovelful of concrete to fill depressions.

Bull float or darby. A bull float is basically a wide, flat board attached to a long handle. It is pushed and pulled across the concrete to give it an initial smoothing and to make sure the coarse aggregates are pushed below the surface. A darby does the same thing for smaller projects, such as a sidewalk. To use the bull float, push it away from you with the leading edge slightly raised so it will not dig in. Pull it back in the same manner with the leading edge raised. Overlap each pass with the float or darby until you have covered the entire pour.

Edging. Both before and after using the bull float, use your trowel to separate the concrete from the form boards by cutting along each form.

If forms are to be removed after the concrete has hardened, smooth and round the top edges of the concrete with an edging tool. This will not only improve the appearance, but the rounded edges will not readily crack or chip off.

Control joints. Concrete will swell and shrink with the seasons, resulting in irregular cracks unless you install control joints. In patios, place control joints every 10 square feet. In walks, put control joints at intervals of 1½ times the width of the walk. If you use divider boards in the patio or walk, they will serve as control joints. Otherwise, cut the control joints with a jointing tool, using a straight board on the concrete as a guide. Control joints are not necessary in slabs that are going to be enclosed, such as garage floors.

Finishes

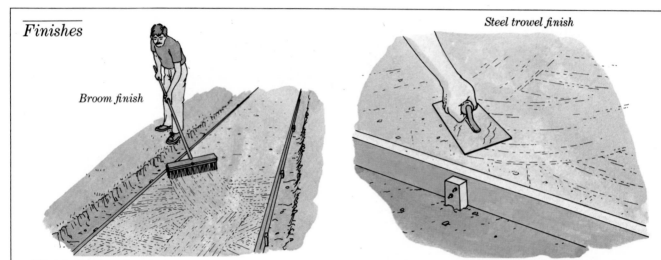

Broom finish

Steel trowel finish

Finish floating. Finish floating is done with different tools, depending on the final texture you want. A broom dragged across wet cement will provide a good nonslip finish for a sidewalk. A wood float provides a smoother surface, but one that still provides sure footing on a wet surface. A steel float is used for a very slick finish. This is good for a garage floor that is out of the weather but should be used with caution on walks and patios because they are quite slippery when wet.

Floating must not be done until the sheen of water on the surface of the concrete has disappeared. This will take only minutes in hot, dry weather and an hour or more in damp, cool weather. Floating too soon will result in a powdery surface on the concrete after it has cured.

Floating should always start with the wood float. Move it back and forth over the concrete with just enough pressure to smooth the concrete but not dig in. If you want a broomed surface, do it after wood floating. You can move the broom straight back and forth or create patterns. If you want a slick surface, use a steel float after the wood float. To float a large surface, you will have to place wide support boards on the concrete on which to kneel. Work backwards, smoothing out the marks from the kneeling boards as you go.

Helicopter finishing

Using a Helicopter

In hot weather, the concrete will harden faster than you can float it, particularly if you are finishing with a steel float. When finishing a large slab, you would be well advised to rent a power finisher rather than attempting to do it by hand. Power finishers, known as helicopters or whirlybirds, are gasoline-powered machines with half a dozen blades that spin around and smooth the concrete. Start using the helicopter when the sheen has disappeared from the surface and it is hard enough to walk on without sinking in.

After the finish work has been completed, cure the concrete by covering it with sheets of plastic weighted at the edges and any seams to trap all moisture. Let the concrete remain this way for about five days for a good cure.

Custom Finishes

Concrete can be finished in so many different ways that you may not realize at first that it is concrete. Several of these different and attractive finishes are described here.

Exposed aggregate. With an exposed-aggregate finish, the surface of the concrete is coated with small stones. The quality of exposed aggregate is directly related to the quality and beauty of the stones. Choose them carefully, for both texture and color. If you can't find them locally, check at a nearby masonry yard.

When making an exposed-aggregate surface, you must divide your concrete project into manageable segments, or some of it may harden before you can work in the aggregate. The first step in exposed aggregate is to pour one section of the walk or patio, strike it off, then cut between the forms and concrete.

Next, sprinkle the stones across the concrete until it is well and evenly covered. With a helper, use a long 2 by 6 or flat shovels to press the aggregate into the concrete.

Exposed aggregate finish

After striking off, sprinkle stones on top of the wet concrete.

Press the stones into the concrete with a flat shovel or have a friend help you with a 2 by 6 board.

Use a wood float to press in stubborn stones.

Brush away excess concrete and hose off the concrete film from the exposed stones.

Embed the stones firmly, until you can just see the tops of the stones. Go over them with wood floats, if necessary, to push them down more. When the concrete has fully hardened— usually three to five hours—broom and spray away the excess concrete around the stones. Work carefully with the broom so you do not dislodge stones. The water spray should be strong enough to wash away the concrete loosened by the broom, but not to blast away green concrete. Let the aggregate sit for another couple of hours, then hose off any concrete film on the stones. Cover with plastic and cure.

Patterned concrete. One simple way to add a pattern is to use a push broom on fresh concrete, as already mentioned. Another equally easy way is to sprinkle rock salt over concrete that has just been finish floated. Lightly float the concrete again enough to press the rock salt flush with the surface. The salt will draw moisture from the concrete and dissolve, leaving a pitted surface. This technique should not be used in areas with freezing winters because frozen water in the tiny holes will damage the concrete.

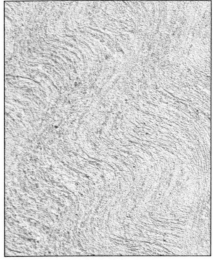

For a textured, nonslip surface, move a broom back and forth on the concrete just after it has been smoothed with a wood float.

Some other easy and appealing patterns can be made by carefully pressing maple or other attractive leaves into the surface of finish-floated concrete. Remove the leaves after the concrete has cured. A pressed-leaf border along a concrete walk is particularly attractive. Other patterns can be made by pressing the ends of different-sized cans into concrete, or by using wood letters or numbers, which are available at hardware stores. Or look for other objects around the house that will produce a unique or interesting shape when pressed into the concrete.

A concrete walk or patio can also be marked with joints so the result looks like flagstone. To do this, use a jointing tool or bend a piece of ½-inch or ¾-inch copper pipe into an elongated S shape. Use one end of the pipe to groove the concrete in the approximate outline of flagstones. One trick of perspective is to make small "flagstones" for walks and large ones for patios. Press down any large pieces of gravel. This tooling process must be done twice: first right after the concrete has been bull floated,

and again after it has been finish floated. Carefully smooth all edges along the tooled grooves, then brush away the concrete crumbs when the walk or slab has hardened. Cover with plastic and cure.

A final method for making patterned concrete is to rent a steel stamping tool that you press into fresh concrete. The base of the steel tool can be shaped like bricks, cobblestone, flagstone, or other patterns.

To stamp concrete, it is best first to measure the base of the stamp you plan to use and adjust your forms accordingly, so that your pattern will come out evenly. Two stamps should be used side by side. You place one, stand on it, then step onto the adjoining one. Impressions in the concrete should be about 1 inch deep. You may want to divide a large pour into several sections because the concrete at one end may be too hard to accept a proper impression by the time you get there. These stamping tools are generally accompanied by jointing tools to smooth out the patterns.

Coloring Concrete

The best way to color concrete is to add the coloring agent to the entire concrete mix, either in a mixer or in a wheelbarrow. This way, the color is mixed throughout the concrete. But for large jobs, this can be expensive. An alternative is to pour uncolored concrete to within 1 inch of the top, then color the concrete mix for the final layer.

A less effective alternative is to sprinkle the coloring agent over the surface of freshly floated concrete. While it is easy enough to sprinkle on the color, it is very difficult to place it evenly and the result may be splotchy coloring. When using this method, place the coloring agent on the concrete, then go over it again with a wood or steel float. Add more color where necessary.

A third way to color concrete is to stain or paint it, using special concrete stains and paints. These should only be applied on concrete that is at least one year old. They barely penetrate the concrete and will soon wear off in average foot traffic.

Stamping concrete

Stamping tool forms pattern.

Flagstone joints in concrete

Use a jointing tool to groove the concrete to look like flagstone.

The earthy red tone of the concrete contrasts nicely with the brown wood and green plants to create a comfortable, relaxing outdoor living area.

For a Leisure Pace— Concrete Molds

Pouring a large patio or walkway entails considerable work, but when you have a big expanse of ground that needs covering, there is an alternative that doesn't require a transit-mix truck. It involves making forms for different-sized paving blocks. The blocks can be virtually any size or shape you want, and they can be colored or finished with patterns or exposed aggregate. Using 2 by 4s, make several forms or use your own design. Paint the inside of each form with old engine oil so they can be removed easily. After the concrete is poured into the forms, strike off the tops with a straight 2 by 4, then smooth the surface with wood or steel floats. When the concrete has hardened, cut between the concrete and form with a trowel and remove the forms. Clean the forms thoroughly before putting them away. Cover the paving blocks with plastic for a week to cure them.

Paver block forms

Octagonal forms can be made by adding small 45-degree pieces across each corner.

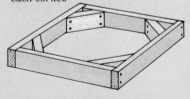

To make hexagonal forms, cut six 2 by 4s the same length with a 30-degree angle cut on each end.

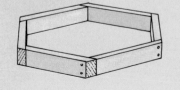

CONCRETE FOUNDATIONS

Many of you have carpentry skills good enough to frame a shed, workshop, cabin, or even a house, but are stymied by the seeming complexities of foundation work. As a result, you may be reluctant to start such a construction project.

Some foundations are considerably easier to form than others. You can form a frame for a slab foundation for an 8-foot by 12-foot workshop, for instance, just by nailing together some 2 by 4s and laying the frame down on level ground.

A foundation for a garage or cabin requires much more preparation. Building a good foundation requires patient work, careful attention to details, and good carpentry skills. The great majority of your time will be spent in framing, squaring, and bracing the foundation forms; the actual pouring and finishing of the concrete will be simple by comparison.

Two types of foundations are covered in this chapter: the slab and the perimeter foundation. Of the two, the slab is simpler to form but must be built on ground that is level or nearly so. The slab is ideal for garages, workshops, and other similar buildings. The disadvantage is that all rough plumbing must be completed before the concrete is poured.

The advantage of a perimeter foundation is that it can be built on irregular or sloping ground. A perimeter foundation also raises the house off the ground and allows easy access to plumbing.

Even a novice can achieve professional-looking results by using the correct techniques and tools. This edging tool forms a round, smooth edge that reduces chipping and cracking.

LAYING OUT THE SITE

Site layout refers to the process used to determine precisely where the outside edge of the foundation will be located. This is done primarily through the use of batter boards.

The structure should be roughly positioned first with a stake at each corner. Stretch a string from stake to stake. Use a carpenter's square to roughly determine each right angle. Then, see how close to square it is by measuring the diagonals. A building layout is square when the diagonal measurements are equal. Move the stakes until the measurements fall within a couple of inches of being square. The actual squaring occurs with the batter boards.

Constructing Batter Boards

Batter boards are located at all four corners and consist of 2 by 4 stakes connected by 1 by 4 boards. Use a framing square to construct the batter boards at 90-degree angles, but don't waste hours being exact. However, make sure the stakes are driven firmly into the ground so the boards are stable. You will be pulling twine on the batter boards, and if they wobble or shift, your work will be inaccurate.

Two things are important about batter boards: where you position them and how you level them. On a small job, where you will be digging the footing ditch by hand, place the batter boards 4 feet out from the rough perimeter strings. If you are going to dig your ditches with a backhoe, either set them 2 feet back so the backhoe operator can reach over them or set them 10 feet back so the operator can maneuver inside them.

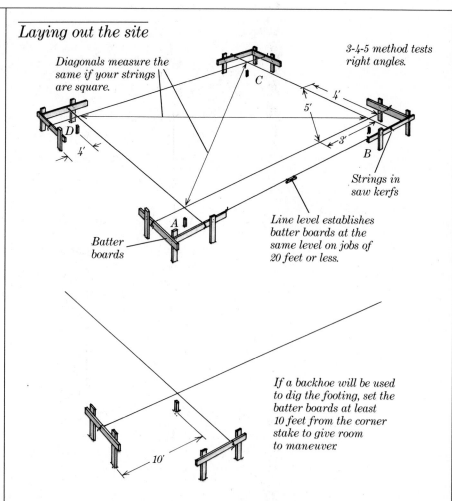

Laying out the site

Diagonals measure the same if your strings are square.

C

D

4'

4'

3-4-5 method tests right angles.

4'

5'

3'

B

Strings in saw kerfs

A

Batter boards

Line level establishes batter boards at the same level on jobs of 20 feet or less.

If a backhoe will be used to dig the footing, set the batter boards at least 10 feet from the corner stake to give room to maneuver.

10'

Leveling Batter Boards

For an accurate layout, the tops of the crosspieces on the batter boards should all be the same height. On small jobs, such as a 12-foot by 16-foot workshop, the tops can be leveled with a line level. Build one batter board, then stretch twine to the other stakes and make a pencil mark on them where level. Nail the crosspieces to the stakes.

On larger jobs, twine cannot be stretched tight enough for accurate leveling. Here you can quickly and efficiently find the level with a transparent plastic hose or a hose leveling attachment found in most large hardware stores. This consists basically of some clear plastic tubing that fits over each end of a hose. To use it, first build a batter board at one corner, using a level to make sure both crosspieces are level. For a poured perimeter foundation, the tops of the crosspieces should be the same height as the top of the foundation wall. Build this first batter board at the highest corner of ground when working on sloping terrain. Fill the hose with water—in fact, let it overflow to make sure no air bubbles are trapped in the hose—then hold one end so the water line is level with the top of the crosspiece. Have a helper take the other end of the hose to the stakes driven at the other corners. Mark each stake at the water line, then nail the tops of the crosspieces flush with these marks.

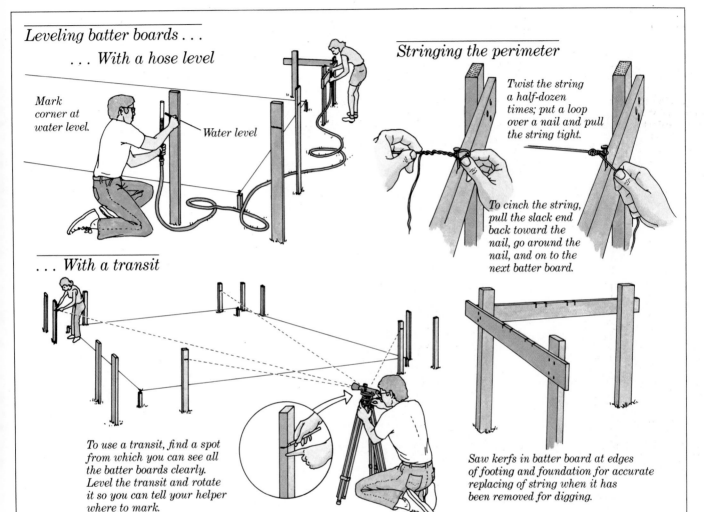

Leveling batter boards...

... With a hose level

Mark corner at water level.

Water level

... With a transit

To use a transit, find a spot from which you can see all the batter boards clearly. Level the transit and rotate it so you can tell your helper where to mark.

Stringing the perimeter

Twist the string a half-dozen times; put a loop over a nail and pull the string tight.

To cinch the string, pull the slack end back toward the nail, go around the nail, and on to the next batter board.

Saw kerfs in batter board at edges of footing and foundation for accurate replacing of string when it has been removed for digging.

Faster and more accurate than the hose device is the transit. This is basically a small telescope that remains perfectly level as you move it. Set the tripod far enough back from the low corner of the building site so that you can see all four corners when you move the transit. Use the bubbles on the sight to level the transit. Move it back and forth and double check that it is still level. Now set the batter-board stakes at all four corners, but do not put on the crosspieces. Starting with the stakes at the highest corner of the site, center the transit sight on one of the stakes. Have a helper mark the stake where the cross hairs are centered.

Turn the transit to each succeeding corner and repeat this process. Nail the crosspieces to the stakes with

the tops flush with the lines, and they will all be level.

Stringing the Perimeter

Once the batter boards are in place, stretch twine between the batter boards to mark the outside edge of the foundation. Stretch the first string above the rough string layout you have on the ground for the south side of the building. Everything else must be square with this line. Drive small nails in the top of the crosspieces and attach the string to the nails.

The twine must be pulled extremely taut to eliminate any sags. To tie off twine on nails in a crosspiece, use the technique shown; then, without cutting the twine, cross over to

the other crosspiece, tie it around the nail, and string the next leg.

Pull the next leg at right angles to the first by using the 3-4-5 method. Do the same on the succeeding legs. Now, to check your work, first measure the building dimensions, then measure the diagonals. Adjust the strings until the diagonal measurements are equal.

Once you have squared the building, cut a shallow notch with a saw underneath each string where it crosses the top of the batter board. This is more accurate than trying to rely on nails, which may bend or come loose. When the strings have to be removed for digging the footing ditch, they can be quickly restrung over the notches.

BUILDING THE FOOTINGS

A footing ditch is required under slab and perimeter foundations. Construction manuals often explain how to lay out the site with batter boards, briefly mention that you should dig the footing ditch, then move on to the next step.

Footing ditches deserve more care. How deep should they be? How wide? What if your ground isn't very level? The answers to these and other questions given here are based on the Uniform Building Code, but local codes may vary, so be sure to check with your local inspector before starting a project. Additionally, if an architect drew up your plans, make the ditch according to the plan's specifications, which should meet or exceed local code requirements.

A footing ditch must be dug in undisturbed soil, not fill dirt. It must be deep enough to reach below the frost line. If you live in an area where the ground does not freeze, the required footing depth is 12 inches for a one-story house and 18 inches for a two-story house.

Perimeter foundation footings must be 12 inches wide for a one-story house and 15 inches wide for a two-story house. One-story houses require a 6-inch-wide foundation wall; two-story houses require 8-inch-wide walls. The footing must be 6 inches thick for a one-story house and 7 inches thick for a two-story house.

The footing ditch around the perimeter of a slab must be 12 inches deep or below the frost line, and 6 inches wide.

Into all footing ditches must be placed ½-inch reinforcing rods, known in the trade as rerod, rebar, or steel. For details on how to hang steel in a foundation, see page 87.

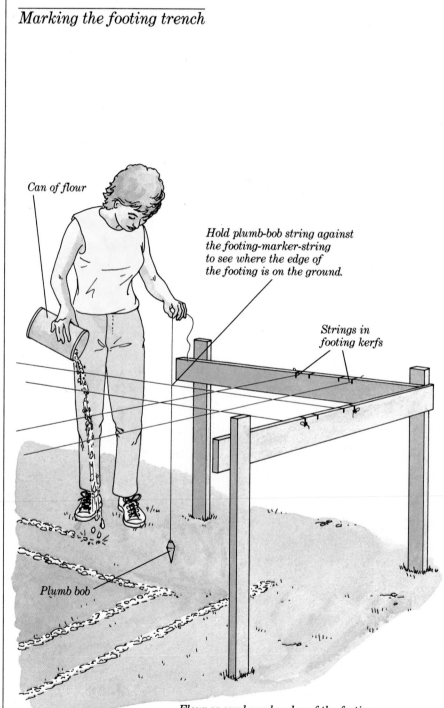

Marking the footing trench

Can of flour

Hold plumb-bob string against the footing-marker-string to see where the edge of the footing is on the ground.

Strings in footing kerfs

Plumb bob

Flour or sand marks edge of the footing and shows your helpers (or backhoe) where to dig.

Digging the Footing Ditch

For all the care you have put into getting the strings placed accurately, the footing ditches are not dug with great accuracy. Work carefully, but the footing may still end up a few inches out of line. However, the foundation wall itself must be placed with great accuracy. With the perimeter strings in place, mark where the footing ditches will be dug.

If a backhoe is digging the footing ditches, you need only mark the outside edge of the footing ditch. The line is marked by dribbling lime or flour from a coffee can. The operator will follow that line with the backhoe bucket. After marking the ditch, remove all the strings so the backhoe can get in there. You can replace the perimeter strings exactly as they were because the saw kerfs still mark the string locations on the batter-board crosspieces.

If you are digging the footing ditch by hand, stretch temporary strings on the batter boards, marking the inside and outside of the footing ditch. For a 6-inch-wide foundation wall, the outside of the footing will be 3 inches outside the perimeter string and the inside of the footing will be 9 inches inside the perimeter string. Use a plumb bob to transfer the string lines accurately to the ground, then mark the ditch outline.

Uneven Ground

Constructing footings for houses on steep slopes is beyond the scope of this book, but it is not uncommon to build a house or cabin on uneven ground. This may mean, for example, that the foundation wall at the high point of ground will be the minimum 16½ inches above grade, but the other end will be 3 feet high. That means pouring a lot of concrete. If practical, the best solution is to have a bulldozer level the ground for you. The alternative is to step the foundation down. Short stud walls, called cripple walls, are then built on each foundation step to bring everything up to level.

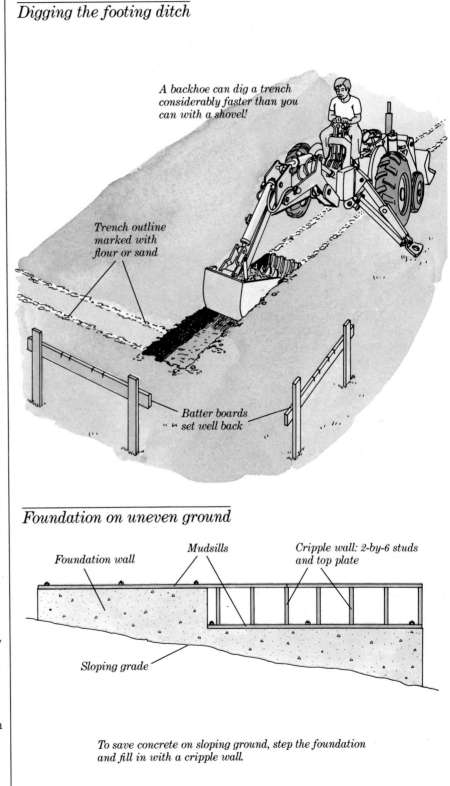

Digging the footing ditch

A backhoe can dig a trench considerably faster than you can with a shovel!

Trench outline marked with flour or sand

Batter boards set well back

Foundation on uneven ground

Foundation wall

Mudsills

Cripple wall: 2-by-6 studs and top plate

Sloping grade

To save concrete on sloping ground, step the foundation and fill in with a cripple wall.

SLAB FOUNDATION

T he slab foundation is a top choice when you plan to build a garage or workshop on relatively level ground. The great advantage of a slab is that once it is poured you are ready to put up walls.

If you live in an area where the ground isn't subject to frost heave and you want a simple 8-foot by 8-foot tool shed in the back yard, you can make the foundation simply by nailing some 2 by 4s together. Once the forms are square and level, brace them every 2 feet with stakes, and fill them with concrete.

For larger and more complex slabs, such as a garage slab, this method is not sufficient. For these slabs, additional construction techniques described below are required, so the slab will withstand frost heaves and support the weight of the building.

A slab foundation involves building a form around the perimeter, pouring concrete, and finishing the surface to the desired smoothness.

After the forms are filled with concrete, cut between the concrete and forms as shown, then remove the forms.

Code Requirements

When building a garage slab, you must submit plans to the building department and obtain a building permit. Here is a checklist of code requirements you generally will have to meet, but you should consult with your building inspector in case local codes differ.

■ The concrete slab itself must be 4 inches thick.

■ A footing ditch must be dug around the perimeter of the slab. The ditch must be 6 inches wide at the base and 12 inches deep, or below the frost line.

■ The footing ditch must contain two layers of reinforcing rod, one about 3 inches from the bottom of the ditch and one about 3 inches from the top of the slab. Where one rod meets another, they must overlap by specific amounts and be wired together. Overlap ½-inch rerod 24 inches and ⅝-inch rerod 30 inches.

■ The top of the slab must be 6 inches above the surrounding soil.

■ Most areas require a 3-inch to 4-inch layer of gravel under the concrete. This keeps the slab off the ground and reduces chances of groundwater soaking through the concrete. If you are laying down gravel, form the slab with 2 by 8 boards, which allows 4 inches of gravel and 4 inches of concrete.

■ Although not required, it's good practice to cover the gravel with 6-mil polyethylene, which keeps moisture in the concrete and thus aids in the curing process. If you don't use plastic, thoroughly wet the gravel before making the pour.

■ A layer of 6-inch-square welded wire must be placed in the slab. The wire should be held off the surface of the gravel by rocks or small blocks so it will be centered in the concrete.

■ Anchor bolts must be placed in the concrete to hold the mudsill. Use ½-inch-diameter anchor bolts that are 10 inches long and embed them 7

inches in concrete. Place them 6 feet on center and not more than 12 inches away from the end of a mudsill. Remember not to place bolts in door openings where there will be no mudsill.

Constructing the Forms

As with any major foundation, first lay out the site with stakes and twine to roughly position the building, then construct your batter boards and place the perimeter strings, as described on pages 80–81. Batter boards for a slab should be built fairly low to the ground so that the string lines will be only a few inches above the top of the form boards. If you are going to have a backhoe dig the footing ditch, place chalk lines on the ground and remove the strings for the backhoe. If you are going to dig the footing ditch yourself, it can be done after the form boards are in place.

Slab foundation (cross section)

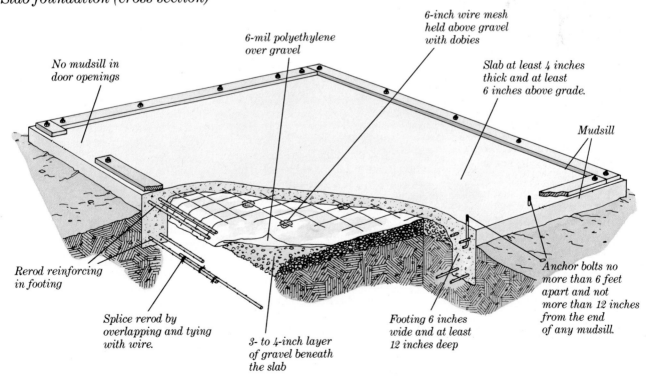

No mudsill in door openings

6-mil polyethylene over gravel

6-inch wire mesh held above gravel with dobies

Slab at least 4 inches thick and at least 6 inches above grade.

Mudsill

Rerod reinforcing in footing

Splice rerod by overlapping and tying with wire.

3- to 4-inch layer of gravel beneath the slab

Footing 6 inches wide and at least 12 inches deep

Anchor bolts no more than 6 feet apart and not more than 12 inches from the end of any mudsill.

Building the forms

Flour marks inside the edge of footing trench yet to be dug

Top of form boards are always made level

Bracing to prevent form bowing

Stakes about every 18 inches

Fill in gaps beneath form boards with scrap lumber and bank dirt against the form for support.

Form Boards

Usually the ground for your slab will not be perfectly level, but this is not a serious problem. The low spots can be filled in with gravel and additional concrete. Start placing the form boards at the highest corner and work toward the low corner. Using a plumb bob, drop a line from where the strings cross at the corner and place the first form board there, with the inside face just under the string. Drive a stake along the outside of the board, and nail the stake to the form board. Place a level on the form board and stake it at the other end. Continue around the perimeter in this fashion, then begin straightening and bracing the form boards.

Sight down a form board to see if it bows in or out. Pull it into line under the string and stake it. Drive stakes every 18 inches along the forms to keep them from bowing out under the weight of the concrete.

At the low side of the slab forms, there may be a gap of a few inches to nearly a foot under the top form board. Fill this gap with additional boards nailed to the stake, then pile dirt against the outside of the forms.

Footing Ditch

With the forms in place, dig the footing ditch according to your local code requirements. After the ditch is completed, hang the steel as described on page 87. With that job

Screed guides

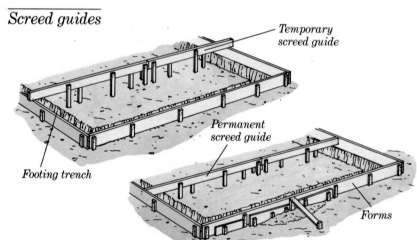

Temporary screed guide

Permanent screed guide

Footing trench

Forms

complete, you are ready to construct screed guides (for large slabs).

Screed Guides

Garages are often 20 or more feet wide, which means you cannot find a board long enough to use as a screed when striking off the concrete. There are two ways to solve this problem. The first is to install permanent dividers in the garage, using either treated or naturally rot-resistant wood. The second solution is to install temporary screed guides that can be used both to level the gravel base for the slab and to strike off the slab itself.

Screed guides are 2 by 4s supported on stakes. Permanent guides must be level with the tops of the forms and, if more than one is used, you must space them equally apart.

The guides should be 8 feet to 10 feet apart, depending on the width of the slab. For a slab 24 feet by 24 feet, for example, place the two screed guides at the 8-foot and 16-foot marks. For temporary screed guides, place one end of the 2 by 4 screed guide on top of the form, level it, and stake it in place. Now, working from the other side, repeat this process so the guides meet at or near the center.

With the screed guides in place, you will need a screed made from 2 by 4s. For temporary guides, nail an "ear" made from a 1 by 2 stake to the end of the screed that will ride on the temporary guide. The other end of the screed rides on top of the exterior form. For center screeds, use ears on both ends of the screed. Temporary screed guides will be removed after the concrete is poured.

Gravel

Add the gravel once all the items above are in place. To level the gravel inside the forms, use a screed made from two 2 by 4s held together with plywood cleats. Screeding the gravel the width of the additional 2 by 4 places the gravel 4 inches below the top of the forms, which is the standard thickness of a garage slab. For thicker slabs, adjust the screed boards accordingly.

Vapor Barriers

A vapor barrier provides protection against water working its way through the concrete slab and helps the concrete cure better. The barrier is made by spreading 6-mil plastic sheets over the leveled gravel. Overlap the sheets by 12 inches. Do your best not to tear the plastic.

Reinforcing Wire

Reinforcing wire is sold in rolls, and you must cut it to fit within your forms. Leave it long enough to reach from form to form, and wire it to the steel in the foundation ditch. Wherever one strip of wire meets another, they should overlap by 6 inches.

The wire should be raised off the ground so it will be in the center of the slab. Place rocks at regular intervals to raise it. Be careful that the wire doesn't bow up so that it would be exposed on the surface.

Hanging the Steel

Steel reinforcing rods must be placed in the footing ditch in two layers, one about 2 inches from the ground and the other about 2 inches below the surface of the finished slab. Where two reinforcing rods meet, they must overlap by 24 inches for ½-inch-diameter rerod and 30 inches for ⅜-inch rerod. Normally, ½-inch rerod is all that is needed in slab foundations. Use tie wire, available at most hardware stores, to wire the steel together. To bend the steel to go around a corner, just put one foot where you want the bend to be, then pull up on the remaining length of rod.

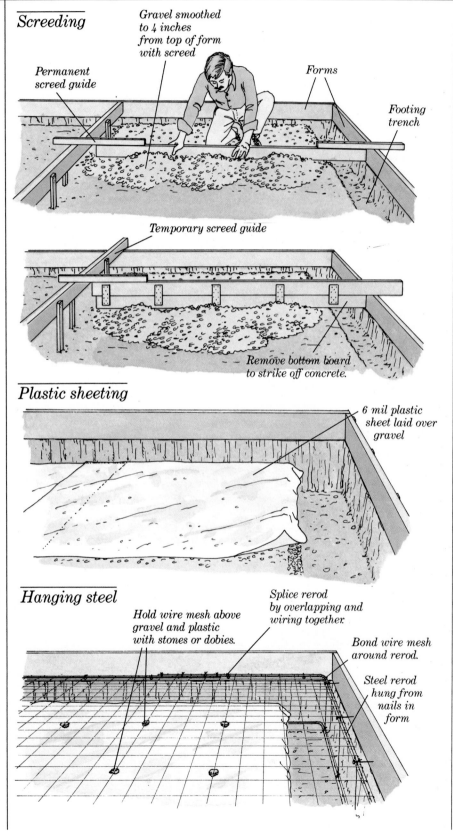

Screeding

Gravel smoothed to 4 inches from top of form with screed

Permanent screed guide

Forms

Footing trench

Temporary screed guide

Remove bottom board to strike off concrete.

Plastic sheeting

6 mil plastic sheet laid over gravel

Hanging steel

Hold wire mesh above gravel and plastic with stones or dobies.

Splice rerod by overlapping and wiring together.

Bond wire mesh around rerod.

Steel rerod hung from nails in form

To hang the steel, drive nails on the inside of the forms, 2 inches below the surface and about 3 feet apart. Using tie wire hung from the nail ends, suspend the bottom layer of steel 2 inches off the ground. Repeat this process for the top layer, hanging it right next to the nails, or resting it on top of the nails if you can. Keep the steel away from the form boards or it will be visible and ineffective.

Pouring and Finishing the Slab

Once you are ready for the concrete, be sure a building inspector first approves your work. The inspector will check that: 1) the footing ditch is deep and wide enough; 2) there is the right amount of steel in place and the overlaps at joints are long enough; 3) the gravel base is in place; 4) the reinforcing wire is laid out; and 5) you have the required number of inches (usually 4 inches)

between the surface of the gravel and the top of the forms.

When the concrete truck arrives, the driver will hook up extension chutes for the concrete. If your slab is wider than about 18 feet or if the driver cannot drive to all sides of the forms, you will have to move concrete to the far corners of the slab by wheelbarrow. It is advisable to have at least two wheelbarrows and a couple of helpers on hand.

Start by pouring the area that is farthest from the transit-mix truck. As you begin filling the footing ditch, watch that the reinforcing rods are not pushed against the forms.

Pour concrete in only one section at a time. When that is done, move to the next area while your helpers screed off the first section. If you place too much concrete to move readily with the strikeoff board, use a shovel to move the concrete. Throw additional concrete into low spots.

When using temporary screed guides, where the strikeoff board must fit between the guides, you cannot saw the strikeoff board back and forth much to settle the coarse aggregates. In this case, it is good to have a jitterbug tamper on hand to settle the concrete. Do not overdo it, however, or you will cause too much separation of water and aggregates.

As work progresses, have a helper use a hammer to rap on the outside of the forms. This causes the concrete to settle smoothly against the forms so no air pockets will be visible when the forms are removed.

After the concrete has been poured and screeded, remove the screed guides and stakes. Work the concrete lightly around the stake holes to fill them in.

As the pour proceeds, keep a close eye on the concrete. In hot weather, the first part may be setting too fast while you are still pouring the remainder. After each section has been screeded, smooth it with a bull float.

Pouring and striking off

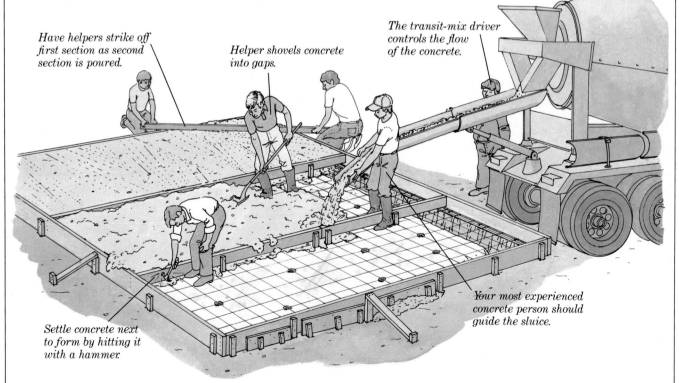

Have helpers strike off first section as second section is poured.

Helper shovels concrete into gaps.

The transit-mix driver controls the flow of the concrete.

Settle concrete next to form by hitting it with a hammer.

Your most experienced concrete person should guide the sluice.

Finishing

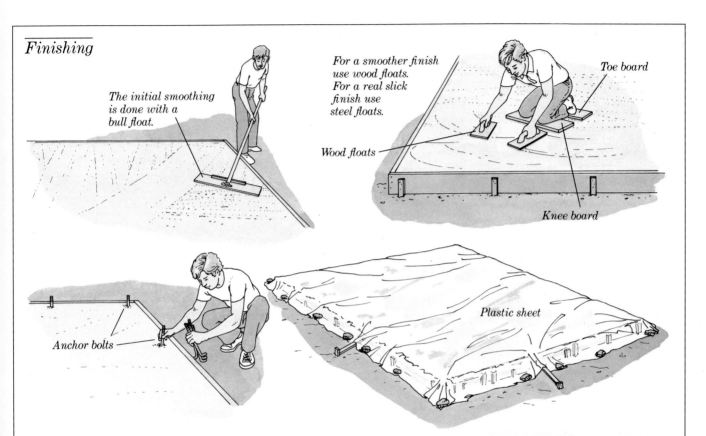

The initial smoothing is done with a bull float.

For a smoother finish use wood floats. For a real slick finish use steel floats.

Wood floats

Toe board

Knee board

Anchor bolts

Plastic sheet

Once the concrete has set enough to place kneeling boards on it without leaving much impression, begin finish floating the slab. Distribute your weight on kneeling boards made from 3-foot-square pieces of ½-inch plywood with 2 by 2s nailed along two edges for handles. Use kneeling boards in pairs, one under your knees and the other under your toes. Go over the surface once with a wood float for a coarse finish, and again with steel floats for a slick finish. For large slabs, use a rented power finisher, as described on page 74.

Before the concrete hardens, take a trowel and cut between the forms and the concrete.

Placing Anchor Bolts

Place the anchor bolts for the mudsill as soon as the concrete has been screeded and bull floated. Using a tape measure as a guide, place bolts 1½ inches away from the edge of the concrete. Push them down until 3 inches remain above the surface.

Keep the bolts straight up and down and in as straight a line as possible.

Place anchor bolts every 6 feet, and one about 6 inches from the end of each mudsill. That means you should know how long your mudsills will be and place one at each end. Do not place the bolts in any door opening. Also, use your tape measure as a guide so you do not put a bolt right where a stud will be placed on the mudsill. However, if that happens, just cut a notch in the base of the stud to fit over the anchor bolt.

If you forget an anchor bolt, drill through the mudsill into the concrete and use an expansion bolt there.

Curing Concrete

Cure the concrete as described on page 74, preferably by keeping it under a sheet of plastic with all the edges and seams weighted to trap the moisture. Otherwise, cover the concrete with straw or burlap and keep it constantly damp.

When Interruptions Occur

A transit-mix truck holds about 8 yards of concrete, and if you are using more than that, you should arrange with the dispatcher for a second truck rather than having the first truck go back for a second load. Ideally, this second truck should arrive just as you have finished spreading the first load, but it is hard to time this exactly. If the second truck has to wait on you, it will cost you money.

When you must wait for a second truck to arrive, keep the area where you stopped the pour continuously wet. Then, when you start pouring there again, work over the old and new concrete with a jitterbug tamper and there should be no visible joint.

Keep all of your tools and wheelbarrows washed and clean during an interruption or the concrete will harden on the equipment.

POURED PERIMETER FOUNDATIONS

The most widely used concrete foundation in this country is the poured perimeter foundation. This type of foundation can be used on level or sloping ground, and has the advantage of keeping the house above the ground.

A perimeter foundation also provides a crawl space under the house for easy access to plumbing, wiring, and heat ducts.

The poured perimeter foundation can be built in several ways. In one style, not very common today, the footing is poured first and allowed to set before the foundation wall is poured. That means the concrete truck has to make at least two trips, which costs more. The method widely used by professionals today is to pour the footing and the foundation wall all at once. This style, known as a stem wall, is described here.

The stem wall is formed with lumber you will later use for the floor joists and rafters. This means you don't have to buy special form material. The joists and rafters will be stained slightly by the concrete, but this doesn't matter because they are hidden from view.

To construct a stem wall, you suspend the foundation wall forms in the footing ditch. As the concrete is poured, it fills the bottom of the ditch, then comes up inside the wall forms.

Constructing the Forms

The perimeter wall is laid out in the standard fashion using batter boards and twine to find the outside of the foundation wall, as described on pages 80–81.

The stem wall is suspended over the footing ditch by hanging the form boards on either 2 by 4 stakes or steel support posts. The steel support posts, which can be rented, are easier to use, particularly if you have to drive them into hard ground.

Support Stakes

Place the outside form boards first, starting with the end wall at the highest corner of the layout. With your perimeter strings in place, begin driving stakes about every 4 feet into the ditch. Since the form boards are 1½ inches thick and the stakes will be nailed to the outside of the boards, use your tape measure to place the stakes 1½ inches outside the perimeter line. When you nail the boards to the stakes, the inner edge should be directly under the string.

One trick for getting steel stakes nearly vertical is to suspend the stake at the top between the tip of your

Stem wall foundation

Drive steel support stakes into the footing trench 1½ inches outside the "outside-of-foundation-wall" string.

thumb and forefinger before you hammer it into the ground. After the form boards are nailed to the stakes, the entire wall will be straightened and braced in position.

A poured perimeter foundation requires sturdy, well-braced forms to hold the concrete. However, the finishing work is easy, since there is no large surface to smooth.

The Form Boards

With the stakes in place, begin nailing up the form boards. This will require two people, one at each end of a board. Start the first board at one corner, with one end of the board extending a foot or so beyond the corner of the string line. The other wall will butt up against this first wall. Pull the board up until it is just a hairbreadth away from the string, but not touching it. Nail through the stake holes into the form board. Keeping the top board perfectly in line with the string, put at least two nails through each stake into the board.

When necessary, drive additional stakes to support the end of a form board and to start the next one that butts up against it. After the top boards are placed along the first end

Building the forms

The top form board almost touches the string.

Add form boards until they reach the approximate top of the footing.

Form braces

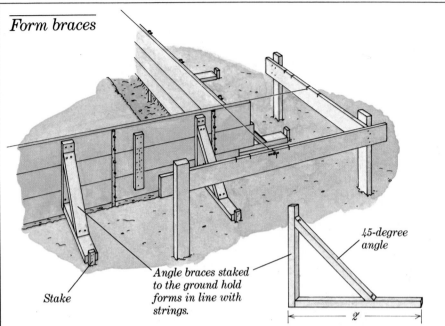

Stake

Angle braces staked to the ground hold forms in line with strings.

45-degree angle

2′

wall, start the second course. Space this course so the ends do not fall on the same stakes as the top course. Pull the second-course boards up tight against the top course and nail through the stakes. The number of courses you must put up will depend on the height of your wall and the width of your boards. The last course should extend into the ditch to approximately the top of the footing. This means the bottom of the lowest form board will be about 6 inches from the bottom of the ditch, which allows a 6-inch-thick footing.

When you come to the first corner, allow the ends of the form boards to extend beyond the string line. Butt the ends of the next wall against the first wall, and nail the two walls together. You will have to cut the bottom board that hangs in the footing ditch, but by not cutting any of the others, you save most of your joist and rafter stock.

Continue placing stakes and boards along each wall in this fashion until the exterior wall is complete.

Straightening and Bracing Walls

At this point, the wall may be up, but it will not be at all straight. You straighten and brace at the same time. Bracing the wall thoroughly can not be overemphasized. You have never really felt sick to your stomach until you have seen a wall suddenly give way, and tons of concrete begin to run out onto the ground.

Braces are made from 2 by 4s. The bottom should be 2 feet long and the upright leg about the same height as the wall. Cut the ends of the diagonal piece at a 45-degree angle, and nail the brace together. You need a brace every 4 feet and at all the corners.

Use these angle braces to straighten the wall. This is done by pulling the wall into line directly under the string, nailing the brace to the wall, and then driving a stake in the ground just behind the end of the brace. Then nail the stake to the brace so it won't slip off the stake under the weight of the concrete.

Additional bracing must be done wherever form boards are butted together without a steel support post on each end, which may happen if you run short of posts. The wall can be braced here by nailing a length of 2 by 4 over the butt joint to prevent the concrete from forcing it apart.

When the exterior wall has been straightened and braced, the next task is to hang the reinforcing rods before you do the interior walls.

Hanging Steel

Steel reinforcing rods must be suspended in the footing and in the foundation wall. One layer of reinforcing rod (normally ½ inch diameter, but check with your building inspector) should be placed in the center of the footing, and another about 2 or 3 inches from the top of the foundation wall. If the wall is more than 18 inches high, a third layer of steel should be hung between the top and bottom pieces.

Reinforcing rod must be bent to go around the footing-ditch corners. To do this, put the rod on the ground, place one foot on it where the bend is to be, then pull the rod up toward you. Or you can drive two wooden stakes firmly into the ground spaced about two inches apart, put the rod between them, and then bend it.

Wherever one length of reinforcing rod meets another, the two must overlap by 24 inches and be tied together with metal tie wire, available in most hardware stores.

If you must cut reinforcing rod, cut about halfway through with a hacksaw, then bend it. It will readily break at that point.

To hang the steel in the forms, drive 16d nails every 3 feet into the forms, about 3 inches down from the top of the forms. Start hanging the steel from the top down, wrapping the wire around the reinforcing rod, hanging it from the nail, and allowing enough wire to tie the one or two more layers of steel below that. Keep the steel away from the forms or they will show through once the form boards are removed.

The Interior Wall

To form the interior wall, first string a line from the batter boards 6 inches inside the exterior wall line. Place the support stakes 1½ inches beyond that line, then begin hanging the form boards in the same manner as you did the exterior wall. More boards will have to be cut for the inside form wall because they cannot overhang like the exterior wall.

Hanging the steel

Suspend rerod from forms with wire hung on 16d nails.

Once the interior wall is hung, it is easier to straighten than the exterior wall, because you tie it to the outside wall with spacers. These spacers, cut from 1 by 4s, should be 9 inches long for a 6-inch-wide wall. The additional 3 inches allow you to nail the spacers to the top of the inside and outside form boards.

A ¾-inch hole is drilled in the center of each spacer and the anchor bolts are suspended there during the pour. Find the center of a pattern board by drawing diagonal lines connecting the corners. Use the pattern board to drill out the other braces. Cut enough of these braces to allow you to place one 6 inches from the end of each mudsill and not more than 6 feet apart.

These anchor bolt supports not only tie the top of the wall securely together, but also space it precisely 6 inches apart.

At the mid-level of the wall, use steel tie straps to further tie the wall together. These straps are narrow steel bands that slip through the joints in the form boards and are held in place by pegs on the outside. After the concrete has hardened, remove the pegs, strip the forms, and snap off the short piece of tie strap sticking out of the concrete.

In addition to all this bracing, still use the triangle braces every 4 feet along the inside wall.

Placing spacers and tie straps

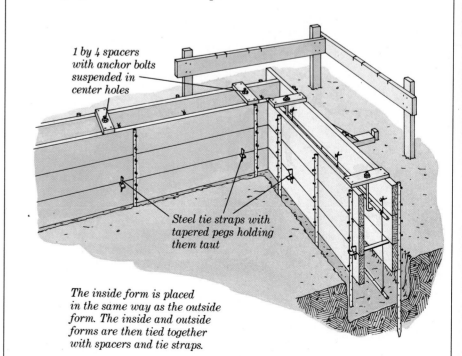

1 by 4 spacers with anchor bolts suspended in center holes

Steel tie straps with tapered pegs holding them taut

The inside form is placed in the same way as the outside form. The inside and outside forms are then tied together with spacers and tie straps.

Some Concrete Tricks

Since you need access to the crawl space under the house after the foundation has been poured, you must form an opening in the wall. Using redwood or treated lumber, make the forms from 2 by 6 material for a 6-inch-wide wall. As shown, it is a three-sided box that is dropped into the formed wall where you want the opening. The bottom of the box should be positioned just above ground level. The open top of the box will be covered by the mudsill. Hold the access form in the wall and nail it in place. Drive a few nails into the uprights to hold the boards in place when the concrete is poured. When pouring, be sure to work the concrete with a shovel so it flows under the bottom of the opening. If girders will be used to support floor joists, the inside of the concrete wall

can be "keyed" to accept the ends of the girders. This is done by cutting a 2-inch length from the end of one girder, or using a similar piece of scrap, and nailing it to the inside form precisely where the girder will fit. Use batter boards set for the interior posts and piers as your guide. The top of the key must be flush with the top of the mudsill, not the top of the wall, so be sure to raise the block 1½ inches above the surface of the wall. When the forms are stripped, the block will have left a 2-inch-deep indentation in the wall where the girder end will fit.

If you are planning on running water, electricity, or heating ducts underground into the house, you will have to form holes in the footing.

This is easily done by placing a length of electrical conduit or plastic drain pipe across the footing ditch before the pour is made. Dig a trench so the pipe extends about 12 inches beyond the footing on each side and can be readily located after the pour is complete. In addition, remember to wrap any conduit or drain pipe in burlap or roofing felt paper before the pour. This provides a cushion around the conduit and prevents the expansion and contraction of the concrete from eventually cutting through the conduit or pipe.

Place the plumbing waste line across the footing ditch in a similar manner before the pour is started.

Additional pipes can be dropped into the footing if you feel it may be necessary to drain water from under the house during the wet season.

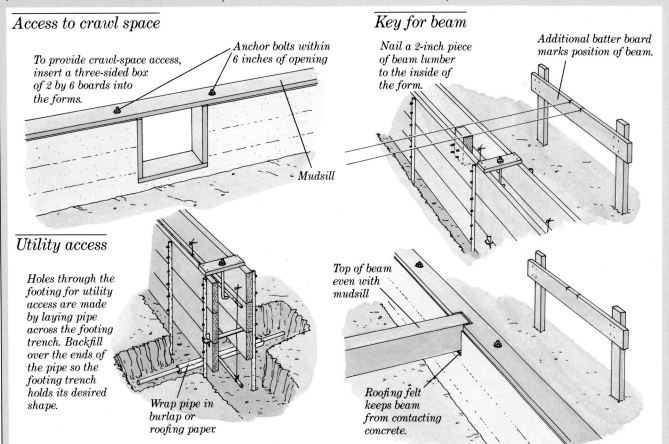

Access to crawl space

To provide crawl-space access, insert a three-sided box of 2 by 6 boards into the forms.

Anchor bolts within 6 inches of opening

Mudsill

Key for beam

Nail a 2-inch piece of beam lumber to the inside of the form.

Additional batter board marks position of beam.

Utility access

Holes through the footing for utility access are made by laying pipe across the footing trench. Backfill over the ends of the pipe so the footing trench holds its desired shape.

Wrap pipe in burlap or roofing paper.

Top of beam even with mudsill

Roofing felt keeps beam from contacting concrete.

Making the Pour

Order the concrete as discussed on page 66. Then, before that big concrete truck arrives, go over your form work one more time, checking that everything is square, the steel is hung, and the access form plus any openings for water and electricity are in place. Then make sure that everything is well braced. Lean over your forms and push out on the walls as hard as you can. If it moves, it isn't braced enough.

Spray or paint the inside of the forms with old crankcase oil shortly before the pour so the forms will pull away from the concrete without sticking and defacing the foundation wall.

You should have a minimum of two and preferably four other helpers on hand. One person must control the chute, working with the truck driver to go around the forms placing the concrete. The other two should be working closely behind the chute operator with long stakes, prodding and poking the concrete to make sure it settles. Another can work behind them with a hammer, rapping on the form walls to chase out air pockets.

Filling the Forms

The chute operator should take the concrete around the forms once to fill the footing ditch until the concrete runs 2 to 3 inches up inside the forms. Don't carry it much higher than this or the concrete will force its way outside the footing ditch.

Once that first pass is made, start the second pass that places the concrete in the foundation wall. If the wall is 18 inches or higher, fill it in two passes. Again, this allows the first layer to harden and reduces the pressure on the forms that would result if you filled the wall all at once. Don't, however, permit any undue delays in passes with the concrete. If one course is allowed to harden completely, the next course will not mix with it and properly adhere at this point, resulting in a weakness known as a cold joint.

Pouring the concrete

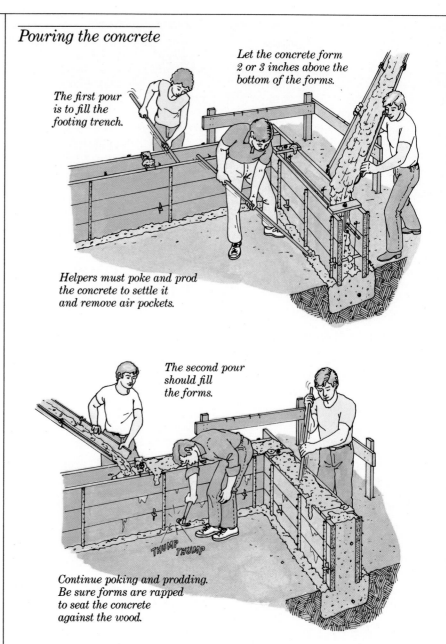

The first pour is to fill the footing trench.

Let the concrete form 2 or 3 inches above the bottom of the forms.

Helpers must poke and prod the concrete to settle it and remove air pockets.

The second pour should fill the forms.

THUMP THUMP

Continue poking and prodding. Be sure forms are rapped to seat the concrete against the wood.

As the chute operator works, the helper directly behind should be watching that the concrete does not force the reinforcing rod against the form boards, which would result in the steel being visible after the forms are removed. If the steel is out of line, it is also not doing its reinforcing job.

The Final Steps

Once the concrete reaches the top of the form, a helper should flatten and smooth the top flush with the top of the form. The helper can use almost anything for this, such as a short length of 2 by 4 or a wood float. A smooth, flat top means the mudsill will lie that much flatter.

Let the forms remain in place for at least 48 hours, and preferably for 72 hours. When you strip the forms, remove any concrete stuck on the boards with a flat-bottomed shovel, so it will not dull your saw blade when you cut them for joists and rafters.

Index

(continues next page)

U.S. Measure and Metric Measure Conversion Chart

	Symbol	When you know:	Multiply by	To find:	Rounded Measures for Quick Reference		
		Formulas for Exact Measures					
Mass (Weight)	oz	ounces	28.35	grams	1 oz		= 30 g
	lb	pounds	0.45	kilograms	4 oz		= 115 g
	g	grams	0.035	ounces	8 oz		= 225 g
	kg	kilograms	2.2	pounds	16 oz	= 1 lb	= 450 kg
					32 oz	= 2 lb	= 900 kg
					36 oz	= 2 1/4 lb	= 1000g (a kg)
Volume	tsp	teaspoons	5.0	milliliters	1/4 tsp	= 1/24 oz	= 1 ml
	tbsp	tablespoons	15.0	milliliters	1/2 tsp	= 1/12 oz	= 2 ml
	fl oz	fluid ounces	29.57	milliliters	1 tsp	= 1/6 oz	= 5 ml
	c	cups	0.24	liters	1 tbsp	= 1/2 oz	= 15 ml
	pt	pints	0.47	liters	1 c	= 8 oz	= 250 ml
	qt	quarts	0.95	liters	2 c (1 pt)	= 16 oz	= 500 ml
	gal	gallons	3.785	liters	4 c (1 qt)	= 32 oz	= 1 l
	ml	milliters	0.034	fluid ounces	4 qt (1 gal)	= 128 oz	= 3 3/4· l
Length	in.	inches	2.54	centimeters	3/8 in.		= 1 cm
	ft	feet	30.48	centimeters	1 in.		= 2.5 cm
	yd	yards	0.9144	meters	2 in.		= 5 cm
	mi	miles	1.609	kilometers	2-1/2 in.		= 6.5 cm
	km	kilometers	0.621	miles	12 in. (1 ft)		= 30 cm
	m	meters	1.094	yards	1 yd		= 90 cm
	cm	centimeters	0.39	inches	100 ft		= 30 m
					1 mi		= 1.6 km
Temperature	°F	Fahrenheit	5/9 (after subtracting 32)	Celsius	32°F		= 0°C
					68°F		= 20°C
	°C	Celsius	9/5 (then add 32)	Fahrenheit	212°F		= 100°C
Area	in.²	square inches	6.452	square centimeters	1 in.²		= 6.5 cm²
	ft²	square feet	929.0	square centimeters	1 ft²		= 930 cm²
	yd²	square yards	8361.0	square centimeters	1 yd²		= 8360 cm²
	a	acres	0.4047	hectares	1 a		= 4050 m²